D0115072

SUMO
WATCHING

edited by S.W.A.

translated by Deborah Iwabuchi

YOHAN PUBLICATIONS, INC.

SUMO WATCHING

Published December 1993
2nd printing January 1995

Originally published by Bronze Publishing Inc. in 1992
English translation copyright © 1993
by Yohan Publications, Inc.

Cover Design:	Eiji Sakagawa
Photographs:	Tsutomu Kakuma
	Takafumi Okuda
Illustrations:	Eiji Sakagawa
	Rakugakisha Inc.
	Ryuji Ikeda
	Akinori Nakamura

YOHAN PUBLICATIONS, INC.

14-9, Okubo 3-chome, Shinjuku-ku, Tokyo, Japan.

Printed in Japan

PREFACE

Sumo is a simple contest, the object being either to throw your opponent down in the ring or out of it. Even people who cannot follow the rules of baseball can join in the dinner conversation on sumo. Children who do not yet understand the point of most sports can instinctively follow a sumo bout. At least in Japan, almost everyone knows about sumo.

But take a closer look at it and suddenly you find yourself in the realm of the unknown. My staff and I found ourselves in this position. Why do *rikishi* have to be so fat? Why do they throw all that salt in the ring? Do *rikishi* get salary bonuses? What level is the *jonidan* rank? Which has the higher status, the east or the west *yokozuna*? How can you buy a ticket for a good seat at a tournament?

The realization of how little we really knew about sumo was what prompted us to write this book. We wanted to write a manual of sumo appreciation. A book by amateurs for amateurs to use to enjoy the sport more.

Bounding with enthusiasm, we set out for the Japan Sumo Association. We were sure that they would welcome our efforts to broaden the appeal of their sport. Instead, we were turned down flat: "We don't think such a book is necessary and we refuse to cooperate with your research." Undaunted, we next visited sumo stables to get some firsthand information. The story was the same. "There is nothing for us to gain from this project." Gritting our teeth, we visited the tea shops that handle tickets for the best seats at the Kokugikan. When we asked the price of *masu-seki* seats, the reply was, "Now why would you want to know that?"

We learned that the sumo society does not give an inch to the press. The prevailing attitude is that nobody without the proper knowledge or connections is welcome to intrude. Was there no place for us fans of sumo? Could we really call it "the national sport?" Thus mumbling under our breath, we trudged off to the Ryogoku Kokugikan early in the morning to wait in line for non-reserved seats. We ran after sumo exhibitions held in tents, and so on.

In our final analysis, however, we decided that sumo has a strong allure and there are many ways to enjoy it. We hope that this book gets you interested in sumo. You can start off by becoming a fan of the Wakanohana-Takanohana brothers or the handsome Terao, and then delve more deeply to discover the essence of the sport and its influence on the life of the Japanese.

Tsutomu Kakuma
During the final days of the
1991 *Kyushu Tournament*

ABOUT THE AUTHOR

Tsutomu Kakuma was born in Ibaraki Prefecture in 1960. He is a freelance writer and editor whose specialties include nature and primary industry; he is also deeply interested in Japanese tradition and folk art. He likes to do his research from a "low angle," and considers himself a jack-of-all-themes (and master of none). His favorite sumo *rikishi* is Mainoumi, whom he calls the "department store of technique."

Kakuma himself aims to become a "manuscript department store" as he searches for new themes to write about. He is also the chairman of the Sports Watching Association (SWA), an organization of and for amateur fans.

CONTENTS

THE RING

WATCHING SUMO ON TV

SUMO IN LONDON

LET'S VISIT THE KOKUGIKAN HALL

KOKUGIKAN WATCHING

EVERYTHING IN SUMO BEGINS ON THE
ROAD

STABLE SUPPORT GROUPS

GLOSSARY OF JAPANESE TERMS

SUMO, SUMO EVERYWHERE

Buddha and Sumo

Sumo may well be the national sport of Japan, but the human instinct to wrestle transcends any temporal or geographical boundaries. Contests of strength with simple rules evolved in a similar fashion in numerous cultures around the world.

The original aim of sumo was simply one of conquest. Over the years, however, sophisticated rules were adopted to remove the blood and gore and it developed into a more peaceful contest of skill. As society creates more and more technologically advanced weapons, sumo remains one of the few tests of true, bare-handed strength.

A 5000-year-old bronze sculpture of two men wearing loincloths and grappling with each other was discovered in the ruins of ancient Babylonia in modern-day Iraq. Similar illustrations were also discovered on a 2500-year-old wall painting from a ruin near the Nile River. The depictions of throws and trips resemble modern Japanese sumo in many ways.

Legend has it that, as a youth, Buddha was renowned, among other things, for his skill in sumo. It is said that many young men tried unsuccessfully to defeat him, but not one was able to even match him. (One wonders at the style of topknot the close-cropped Buddha would have sported.) Reference is actually made to this in *Hongyoku* (a biography of Buddha). It tells how he managed, through his sumo prowess, to win a beautiful princess as his bride.

It is interesting to note that countries as seemingly unrelated as Senegal, Greece, Mongolia, Afghanistan, and Korea have always held simple tests of strength that could be described as sumo.

Oda Nobunaga's Sumo Tournament at Azuchi Castle

Kojiki, the famous Japanese record of ancient history, mentions sumo in its description of the legendary origins of Japan. In the chapter entitled "Giving Away the Country," the gods pitted their strength against each other as they decided how to divide up the country. Another version, *Nihon Shoki*, describes a bout that took place in the Imperial Palace in the year Suinin 7 (23 B.C.) between Nomi-no-Sukune and Taimano-Kehaya. This fight was held to determine whether the Yamato clan or the Izumo clan would have the right to rule. The idea was that the winner would be the gods' choice based on which side they wished to rule the country. After this event, sumo was often used at the palace to determine the will of the gods whether they would grant a bountiful harvest, and so on. This was called *sumo sechie*, and it continued through the Heian era (794-1185).

13

Evidence of the roots of sumo was discovered in Shimane Prefecture in the form of an earthenware vessel dating back to the period of ancient burial mounds. The vessel was in the shape of a sumo wrestler. A *haniwa* figurine found in Wakayama Prefecture of a man in a loincloth with his arms out in front of him is also thought to be a sumo wrestler.

Children's sumo was also popular during the age of *sumo sechie*. In fact, it was very similar to the present scouting systems in that it was used to observe promising young boys with an eye towards raising them to be wrestlers. When wars between the Genji and Heike clans eclipsed the power of the emperor and the society switched from imperial to *samurai* rule, *sumo sechie* became obsolete. The sport reemerged, however, in the form of tests of strength between *samurai*. The emphasis on its entertainment value also grew. During the Kamakura era, command matches were often held for the Shogun; this was called *joran* sumo. Oda Nobunaga, the famous feudal lord, was especially fond of sumo. It is said that he once gathered 1500 men for a tournament at Azuchi Castle.

During the Kamakura era, street, or *tsuji*, sumo gained popularity in provincial towns. However it was frowned upon by the authorities because rowdy spectators (along similar lines as today's infamous soccer hooligans) often incited brawls and other disturbances. As a result, there were frequent bans on sumo.

THE BOUT BETWEEN NOMI-NO-SUKUNE AND TAIMA-NO-KEHAYA

The bout between Nomi-no-Sukune and Taima-no-Kehaya described in *Nihon Shoki,* an ancient historical record, was part of a dramatic struggle for power as well as the story of a fight between the forces of good and evil. In the Suinin (29 B.C.-70 A.D.) era, in the city of Yamato (what is now Nara), there lived a violent man of superhuman strength named Taima-no-Kehaya. This was an age where strength was power, and Taima had little else to recommend him other than his physical prowess. Leaders were terrorized and realized that if nothing was done to control him, the imperial system would be in jeopardy. They finally decided to hold a contest to determine the "strongest man in Japan." His opponent was Nomi-no-Sukune from Izumo (the present-day Shimane). He too was a man of renowned strength, but, in contrast to Taima, he was said to be a very gentle man. Nomi won, of course. He threw Taima to the ground, breaking his bones and rendering him unconscious. He died shortly thereafter.

Stables Began in the Edo Era

When Tokugawa succeeded in unifying the country during the Edo era (1600-1867), the workforce was flooded by *samurai* who found themselves out of work during peace time, with their only marketable skill the strength they had gained through battle. Some eventually banded together to form groups of wrestlers, ostensibly to raise money to rebuild Buddhist temples. These groups of *samurai* evolved into professional sumo wrestlers.

Between 1757 and 1792, sumo stables and tournament systems were established in both the present-day Kansai and Tokyo areas. The large number of wrestlers on retainer kept this system profitable for quite a long time, and many current sumo stable names originate from this.

The Edo-era stables lost the support of the military-run government after the emperor was reinstated as the leader of the country during the Meiji Restoration. Sumo was again forced to make structural changes, with stables even being re-established as "fire-extinguishing crews."

In 1884, the emperor began holding sumo command performances, since which it has continued as a popular sport. (The Showa emperor, Hirohito, was well-known as an enthusiastic fan, and he was a familiar sight at Tokyo tournaments at the Kokugikan Hall.)

In 1926, the separate systems in the east and west were merged, becoming the organization now known as the Japan Sumo Association, and sumo was finally established as the national sport.

Women Wrestlers

Sumo society forbids women from even entering the ring. History, however, shows that it has not always been a totally male sport. *Nihon Shoki* records the ladies-in-waiting of Emperor Yuryaku being ordered to tie on loincloths and wrestle in the year 469.

History also records an incredibly powerful Buddhist nun who took on the men during sumo *kanshin* in Kyoto during the reign of Toyotomi Hideyoshi. Chinese history also contains several instances of female sumo, including some public events. Even Marco Polo's record of his travels in the orient mentions a beautiful princess who wrestled all the men who wanted to marry her, beating them off one by one.

Animal Sumo

Not content to limit sumo to human beings, Japanese throughout history have also enjoyed animal fights. Other cultures must certainly look at us as "sumo freaks."

Chicken Fights

Chicken fights go way back. Records of "chicken combinations" during the age of Emperor Yuryaku (456-479) can be found in *Nihon Shoki*. (This was also the emperor who made his ladies-in-waiting wrestle. He must have been a particularly enthusiastic fan.)

Chicken fights were popular at the imperial court during the Nara (645-794) and Heian eras. They were a favorite entertainment for child emperors and were performed as part of a children's festival at the palace. During the Edo era gamecocks from Southeast Asia were brought in and the sport became a form of gambling, and was subject to frequent bans. Chicken fights are now viewed as inhumane, but are still recognized customs in some areas.

Bullfights

In Spain, bullfights are a battle between man and beast. In Japan, however, they are contests between the bulls themselves. In the old days, bullfights were called "meetings of horns," and the retired Emperor Goshirakawa is recorded, to have witnessed such a bout in 1178.

Rules of the Ring
for Chicken Fights

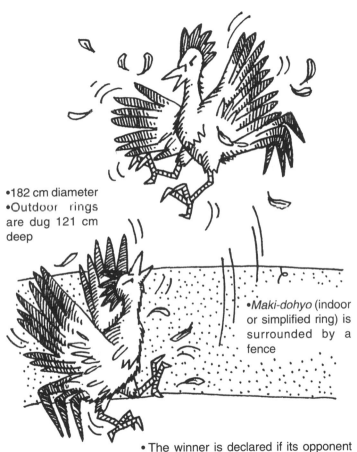

•182 cm diameter
•Outdoor rings are dug 121 cm deep

•*Maki-dohyo* (indoor or simplified ring) is surrounded by a fence

• The winner is declared if its opponent loses the will to fight and curls up to rest, or
• if it drives its opponent out of the ring a total of three times

19

Bullfights were held in cattle-raising districts with the presumed object of finding out which breeds were superior to others. It may be because of this that current contenders in bullfights are quite large. Bullfights are still held on Hachijojima Island and in Uwajima in Shikoku. I was surprised to learn that around the turn of the century, bullfights were held as attractions at the Ryogoku Kokugikan Hall in Tokyo.

Dog Fights

There have been many countries throughout history, which at some stage, have viewed dog fighting as a sport. During the Kamakura era (1192-1333) dog fighting was particularly popular amongst the Samurai. These dogs were bred combining native dogs (Tosa) with pointers, bull dogs, great danes and mastiffs to develop the Tosa fighting dog. Tosa dog fights have a banzuke ranking system based on that of the Sumo ranking system, the dogs also wear the ceremonial rope and all high-ranking dogs wear colorful kesho mawashi aprons.

Insect Sumo

Many Japanese will remember pitting beetles against each other sometime during their childhood. Atlas beetles, especially, have impressive horns that were made for battle. During summer male beetles fight each other for tree sap or for the favors of a female. There are areas of Southeast Asia where beetle fights are a popular gambling object.

Other Animal Sumo

Kappa

The mythical river-dweller *kappa* loved sumo. Legend has it that *kappa* would invite passersby to join him for a bout of sumo, and woe to any who accepted. *Kappa* would drag his opponent into the river and pull out their anus. This rather improbable choice of trophy most likely stems from the fact that when a person drowns, the muscles in the anus loosen. (By the way, a drowned body is referred to in Japan as a "Dozaemon." This was the name of an Edo-era wrestler who was very fat and had an unusually pale complexion. I would feel sorry for him except that his name has lived on longer than those of most *yokozuna*).

Back to *kappa* ; one of his features was a bowl on the top of his head. As long as water remained in the bowl, *kappa* had the strength to overcome any opponent. Once the water was gone, however, even a child could beat him. This one weakness is what has made him one of the more "lovable" of mythical beasts.

Rules for Sumo Games

Paper doll Sumo

Paper doll sumo, too, has a long history. A wooden version of something very much like it was dug up among the ruins of the ancient capital in Nara. Sumo dolls made of paper were popular during the Edo era. This type of game is a sign of how long the sport has permeated the lives of the Japanese.

There is a book by Yoshiyuki Tokugawa entitled *Makeru na! Kamizumo* (Win at Paper Sumo) (Rokkyo Shuppan ¥1736). The author is the founder of the Japan Paper Sumo Association. As you may well imagine, it is not a particularly large group, but it has no less spirit behind it than does the Japan Sumo Association.

Makeru na! Kamizumo carefully lays out the rules for paper sumo. The wrestlers are made of paper, and the dimensions are given in the illustration on the right. Cut out the dolls and fold them down the center at a 45 degree angle. Then bend the legs back and forth to make them pliable. Paper sumo enthusiasts call this action "stamping" after the way human wrestlers stamp to loosen up when they enter the ring.

The ring is made of sand paper and has a diameter of 12 cm. It is held up off the board using plastic erasers. Finally, the wrestlers are set in a clinch in the middle of the ring. Their feet are cut at an angle to prevent them from being able to stand alone. It is an important principle of paper sumo that the contenders cannot stand until they are locked together.

Official Paper Sumo

Making the Ring (cardboard)

12 cm

fasten here

sandpaper

width of "barrels" 0.5cm

nail

about 60 mm

39 mm or less

34 mm or less

35 mm or more

20 mm

plastic erasers

14 cm

hole for nail

Lock wrestlers together

Tap with fingers here

The "referees" then tap the east and west sides of the board to get the opposite side to keel over first. Paper sumo is even more fun if you give your wrestlers names and draw up a ranking chart.

If you happen to visit the Ryogoku Kokugikan Hall, you might enjoy purchasing a cut-out paper sumo set at a souvenir stand.

Arm Sumo

Almost everyone has arm wrestled at one time or another, and the rules are included here for reference.

Elbows are placed in the middle of the table and hands firmly grasped. Contenders put all their strength into pushing their hands down in a natural, forward direction, and, in the process, pushing that of their opponent backwards. If players are of equal height and strength, each grasps a corner of the table with their free hand. Forcing your opponent's fist down on the table for the count of three is the object. If strength is unbalanced, the stronger of the two can grasp the wrist of his or her opponent, or take some other measure to create a handicap.

Thumb Sumo

Opponents lock fingers together keeping their thumbs free. The object is to lock down on your opponent's thumb until the count of ten. There are various possible dodging and thrusting moves, or the famous reversal, in which you manage to get your thumb out from under your opponent's and then pounce down on it before he or she realizes what has happened. An automatic loss

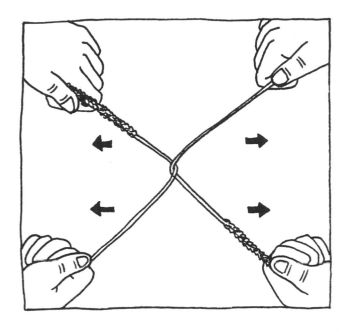

goes to a contender whose forefinger mistakenly joins the action.

Weed Sumo

This is a simple game that Japanese children enjoy playing with a long stemmed weed called a broad-leaved plantain. First, players have to pick a weed. Those that grow in a sunny spot are stout, strong wrestlers. Ones that are of a dark-green color and very fibrous-looking are best. One tactic is to chew on your stem a bit to make it more flexible. Then wrap your weed around that of your opponent (see illustration) and pull. The first one to break is the loser. When two unusually-strong stems face off, the pullers may find their whole bodies involved in the contest.

Oshikura Manju

Another traditional children's game. A circle is drawn on the ground and several players lock arms with their backs to each other. Each tries to push all of the others out of the ring using their backsides. Players are eliminated as they are forced out. Use of arms and legs is prohibited in this generic form of shoving sumo.

Push-and-Pull Sumo

Two people face each other with toes just about touching. The object is to use your hands to push and/or pull your opponent off balance and force them to move their feet.

SUMO THROUGHOUT HISTORY

300 A.D.

The first sumo bout on record; the contest of strength between Nomi-no-Sukune and Taima-no-Kehaya described in *Nihon Shoki*.

1624 (Kan-ei 1)

Said to be the year in which Akashi Shiganosuke was proclaimed the first *yokozuna*.

1789 (Kansei 1)

Tanikaze and Onogawa were the first *rikishi* to go and receive their *yokozuna* licenses from sumo trustee Yoshida in Kumamoto. (To this day, *yokozuna* still visit Yoshida's descendants to receive their licenses.)

1793 (Kansei 5)

At the *sekiwake* rank, Raiden Tameemon won his first tournament.

1909 (Meiji 42)

In June, the first permanent arena for sumo was built in Tokyo's Ryogoku district. At the opening ceremony, sumo was first proclaimed the "national sport" *(kokugi)* of Japan; thus the building was named Kokugikan (hall of the national sport). Up until this time, sumo was held in an outdoor ring and bouts could only be held on sunny days. It would often take up to a month to complete a ten-day tournament.

1914 (Taisho 3)

Tachiyama, Otori and other *rikishi* make an exhibition tour to Hawaii.

1915 (Taisho 4)

Umegatani, Nishinoumi, etc. make an exhibition tour to the U.S.A.

1917 (Taisho 6)

Kokugikan Hall destroyed in fire. Rebuilt in 1920.

1923 (Taisho 12)

In September, Kokugikan Hall destroyed in a fire in the aftermath of the Great Tokyo Earthquake.

1928 (Showa 3)

Time limits placed on bouts. First live radio broadcasts of tournaments.

1945 (Showa 20)

Kokugikan Hall destroyed in air raids on Tokyo; requisitioned by GHQ after Japan's defeat in World War II.

1952 (Showa 27)

In April, Kokugikan Hall returned to the Japanese.

1953 (Showa 28)

May 28. NHK makes the first live television broadcast from Kokugikan Hall.

1954 (Showa 29)

Opening ceremony for Kuramae Kokugikan Hall in September.

1958 (Showa 33)

Name of Great Japan Sumo Association changed to Japan Sumo Association. Six-tournament year established.

1965 (Showa 40)

Taiho, et al, make exhibition tour to the USSR.

1972 (Showa 47)

At the Nagoya Tournament, Takamiyama becomes the first non-Japanese *rikishi* to achieve a tournament victory.

1973 (Showa 48)

Exhibition sumo held in Beijing and Shanghai to commemorate normalization of Sino-Japan relations.

1985 (Showa 60)

Opening of the new Kokugikan Hall in Ryogoku.

1987 (Showa 62)

The Hawaiian *rikishi* Konishiki becomes the first non-Japanese to reach *ozeki*-rank.

1991 (Heisei 3)

Five-day exhibition grand sumo tournament at the Royal Albert Hall in London.

1992 (Heisei 4)

Akebono and Musashimaru, both from Hawaii, are awarded *ozeki* and *sekiwake* ranks respectively.

1993 (Heisei 5)

After his second consecutive tournament victory, Akebono is the first non-Japanese *rikishi* to achieve *yokozuna* status.

BASIC KNOWLEDGE ABOUT SUMO

The Sumo World

Baseball and sumo are the two favorite sports of the Japanese. Compared with the relative freedom of professional baseball players, old-fashioned customs long-abandoned by the population at large still bind sumo wrestlers; they must comply to a rigid code of behavior. And, while the private lives of popular baseball players are available for public consumption in sports newspapers and on daytime television, the structure of sumo society and the lives of the *rikishi* are a mystery even to the most dedicated Japanese fans. The Japan Sumo Association maintains the status quo by refusing to cooperate openly with reporters, turning a cold shoulder to all but a few select journalistic intermediaries.

Behind every successful *rikishi* is an anonymous organization of patrons called *tanimachi*. While it is generally known that they reward their preferred *rikishi* with generous "donations," the source of these donations are never revealed in order to avoid possible embarrassment to the patrons. To the Western observer this may seem a dubious practice. To the Japanese, however, this is not a contentious issue. In fact, the sumo world has always protected the identity of its patrons. Rather than expose the sources of their donations (biting the hand that feeds it as it were), both parties would prefer to maintain this unspoken interdependence.

More than just being a sport, sumo is also a cultural showpiece of sorts, and has been for most of its history. *Rikishi* can be likened to actors; you might even call them male *geisha* in that they are obliged to entertain and please their benefactors. Powerful leaders and lowly citizenry alike have always been enthralled by the novelty and the mystery of these giants, enjoying it as a show as much as a sport. Often *rikishi* are appointed to carry out Shinto rituals for plentiful crops and national peace, indicating not only their tremendous popularity as sportsmen, but also their religious role.

In this age of democracy, equality, and philanthropy, nothing could be more incongruous than sumo. Topknots, loincloths, the elaborate ring-entering ceremony, as well as the ceremonies of salt-throwing and the offering of strength-giving water all contribute romantic images to this sport. Yet the hard facts of the matter are that one change in ranking turns a *rikishi* into a servant to his former peers. This humiliation is accompanied by a substantial drop in income. Like it or not, the sumo world is essentially Japanese, reflecting the strict hierarchy that is still very much in evidence in Japan today.

On the other hand, no one would welcome the day sumo opened its doors to society at large and modernized at the expense of its mystique. If *rikishi* were allowed to cut, style and dye their hair any way they pleased, what would there be to distinguish them from professional wrestlers? What would happen to the uniquely-Japanese atmosphere engendered by the Kokugikan Hall if fans started ringing bells and forming human waves? The sport may as well be moved to a baseball stadium.

One can only hope that sumo remains the stubborn, rigid institution that it is.

The Sumo World is Radical

There is nothing more callous than the sumo world. Without talent, a *rikishi* may find himself the personal valet *(tsukibito)* of a wrestler much younger than himself. The ranking list *(banzuke)* decides everything.

As conservative as sumo is, it is also radical in its exclusive emphasis on talent and its flouting of the Japanese custom of respect for age. In this respect, sumo can also be considered egalitarian.

During the Edo era, the stable *(sumo-beya)* system was established. All *rikishi* are members of one of forty-odd stables, each operated by a stablemaster *(oyakata)*. Sumo

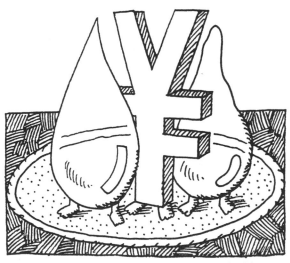

It takes a lot of sweat to make any money in this sport.

is not just a competition between individuals, but also one between rival stables. Once a *rikishi* joins a particular stable, he will never change to another, nor will he be selected to wrestle against a stablemate, except in the case of a tie for tournament championship.

Stables are in the business of getting as many talented *rikishi* into the ring as possible. As well as paying a salary to stablemasters, the Japan Sumo Association also pays for the support of each *rikishi* in the stable. Once a *rikishi* reaches the rank of *juryo* and earns the title *sekitori*, the association adds an incentive payment to his support. The private support groups *(koenkai)* also expand with the prominence of a stable. This increases the reach of the stable network, making it easier to discover new talent. Clearly, the power of a stable lies in the number of its *rikishi*.

A Walk Through the Career of a Sumo Wrestler

What if there was a board game called "The Game of Sumo Life"? What happens to a *rikishi* between apprenticeship and his appointment to *yokozuna*? Below are some ideas....

Scouting Step 1: Discovery

The stablemaster hears about a large boy with potential. Most of this information comes by way of the support group grapevine, although, recently, some stables are rumored to have put help wanted ads in newspapers!

OUT

Adequate in size, but unfortunately lacking in skill.

GO

Scouting Step 2: Convincing the Parents

Because society has always viewed sumo as a spartan life, it is the job of the stablemaster and his scout to reassure concerned parents that notoriously harsh conditions have eased up to some degree.

"Is it true boys get fed nothing but rice?" The stablemaster denies it with great sincerity.

"That was long, long ago. It could NEVER happen nowadays!"

The biggest recruiting problem these days is that sumo life appears less and less attractive because families are not as poor as they used to be and many a prospective *rikishi* is the only child in the family.

Promises of fame and glory are backed up by efforts on the part of the support groups, local stable connections and any relations in the area. Some parents have been known to ask for contract money.

OUT

The doting parents are too worried about the hardships their boy would encounter, and negotiations break down.

GO

Scouting Step 3 : Convincing the Boy

If the parents agree to the conditions proposed by the stablemaster, all that remains is the boy's decision. Being a master of his trade and a hero of recent vintage, a few well chosen remarks on the stablemaster's part about potential success, and the boy is a willing recruit.

One well-known story of the recruitment of a famous wrestler is that of Kitanoumi who was wooed by a pair of socks hand-knitted by the stablemaster's wife. Chiyonofuji gave in when he was promised a trip by airplane to Tokyo from his home in Hokkaido.

OUT

The boy just can't bring himself to cut the apron strings and ends up staying home.

GO

The Apprentice Arrives at the Sumo Training School

The first step for new arrivals is the new-apprentice examination. Requirements for these beginners are graduation from junior high school (nine years of compulsory education), a height of at least 173 cm, and a minimum weight of 75 kg. Most young men nowadays pass this inspection easily. In the old days, however, *rikishi* took drastic steps to pass. They might have a senior apprentice hit them over the head to add a lump's worth of height, or stuff themselves with tofu and water before weighing in. Mainoumi, a current *rikishi* of the

OUT

The original enthusiasm is replaced by the desire to have a good time. The budding apprentice quits without a second thought.

Dewanoumi stable, passed his height requirement thanks to a lump on his head (rumor has it that he even had it filled with silicone—now that's tenacity!) Once this test is over, an apprentice is registered with the Japan Sumo Association as a *rikishi*.

This is followed by six months at the Sumo Training School. The regimen here includes written theory as well as sumo training. Training consists of running, stamping, splits, push-ups, sliding, shuffling, falling, rushing, etc. Studies include anatomy, law, *shigin* (a classical form of singing), calligraphy, sumo history, and so on.

GO

OUT

The Bottom of the Ladder 1 : The New Apprentice

The hard work finally begins. Newcomers often experience a form of culture shock as their training *(keiko)* begins in earnest. It wouldn't be going too far to write the word "knuckles" and read it "senior apprentice." Before and after merciless training sessions, the new apprentice finds himself a slave to his seniors, doing an endless stream of chores and errands. The shock doubles and triples as the new *rikishi* learn the cold-blooded reality of the ranking system. The stablemaster, who had been a kind, attentive scout, is now more terrifying than anybody else. Half of all apprentices quit after the first year.

Unable to cope with the harsh life-style of the stable, the young rikishi makes one escape attempt too many.

GO

The Bottom of the Ladder 2 : Reaching *Sekitori*

A *rikishi* is referred to as a *sekitori* when he reaches the rank of *juryo*. This is also the point where he starts receiving a monthly salary. This means that a *rikishi* will never be considered a pro unless he reaches this point. *Rikishi* below this rank are not even permitted to marry. He must win his way through the *jonokuchi, jonidan, sandanme,* and *makushita* ranks before he receives his ticket into *juryo*. Those who wrestle during college are considered to have attained a certain level of skill and are allowed to enter at the *makushita* rank. It still takes them four or five tournaments to reach *juryo*.

OUT 1

Quit while you're ahead and open a *chanko-nabe* restaurant.

OUT 2

Life after retirement does not go well either, and the ex-*rikishi* never recovers from the failure.

GO

Sekitori 1 : *Juryo*

At long last, he is promoted to *juryo*. The *rikishi* finds his name in the newspaper and even hears it on TV. He finally gets a salary and is assigned a junior *rikishi* to do his bidding. For the first time, he is able to appreciate the fact that he is in the sport. The juryo rank, however, is located precariously on the border between the heaven and hell of the sumo world. There is still a long road ahead to becoming a *yokozuna*.

OUT

The *rikishi* cannot win in the *juryo* rank and is demoted to *makushita*.

GO

OUT

Sekitori 2 : *Maegashira*

Moving up gets more difficult as the quality of the competition increases. No longer does he find himself gaining a rank at regular intervals, and *rikishi* below him are hot on his heels. Still, he has a sense of accomplishment and even acquires a following. Some, however, begin to feel their age at this stage.

After an injury and consequent demotion to *juryo*, a scandal (such as taking a bribe to lose) puts the *rikishi* in an awkward social predicament.

GO

Sekitori 3 : The Top Three Ranks *(Sanyaku)*

The *rikishi* wins a gold star for defeating a *yokozuna*, takes one of the three special tournament prizes: the Fighting Spirit Prize, the Technique Prize, or the Outstanding Performance Prize, and is promoted to *komusubi*. The barriers of *sekiwake* and *ozeki* are still ahead. Fans and the media become more attentive. Both wins and losses are points for speculation. The pressure is on.

OUT

Health problems become aggravated and there are calls for retirement.

GO

GO

Sekitori 4 : *Yokozuna*

Representatives of the Sumo Association arrive at the stable with news of promotion to *yokozuna*. Supporters surround the new grand champion with the traditional *banzai* cheer. The hometown goes crazy in celebration. The pressure on a *yokozuna* is great, but he has been chosen for his talent and spiritual maturity. Only one in 350-400 *rikishi* achieve this rank. Promotion to *yokozuna* is comparable to the chances of becoming Prime Minister. Each *yokozuna* is a legend in his own lifetime.

OUT 1

The *yokozuna* skips a tournament to rest up, but finds himself overpowered by younger opponents. He finally retires a weak champion.

OUT 2

Trouble arises and the *yokozuna* flees the sumo association to become a professional wrestler.

GOAL

Retire a star and become an elder of the Japan Sumo Association.

What is a Stable and What Does the Stablemaster Do?

Not even *yokozuna* can retire and automatically become stablemasters.

Before they retire from active participation in sumo, stablemasters have to buy an "elder stock." There are a total of 105 of these. (Exceptions being those of former *yokozuna* Taiho and Kitanoumi who were given possession of one-generation stock, meaning that they cannot be sold to other elders after the present owners retire. The current total, then, is 107). The owners of the stock are known as "successors to the name" and are members of the Japan Sumo Association. They participate in the operations of the association and are paid a salary until they reach the retirement age of 65. Their formal title is Trustee of the Japan Sumo Association. Owners of the stock are allowed to run stables. Professional requirements for becoming an elder are to have competed in one entire tournament as a *makuuchi rikishi* (*maegashira* or higher ranking), or twenty straight tournaments at the *juryo* rank, or a total of twenty-five tournaments as a *rikishi* of any ranking. The gate is suprisingly wide.

Support Paid to Stables by the Sumo Association
(current as of October, 1991)

Rikishi training (per month, per apprentice)	¥55,000
Rikishi support (per tournament, per *rikishi*)	25,000

Training support (per tournament)	*Yokozuna*	¥300,000
	Ozeki	200,000
	Sekiwake, Komusubi	100,000
	Maegashira	50,000
	Juryo	30,000
Stable maintenance (per tournament)		
Training/support per wrestler per Tokyo tournament		100,000
For other tournaments per wrestler		85,000
Training session operations (per tournament)		
per *Sekitori* (*Juryo* ranking and above)		43,500
per apprentice		30,500

Wrestlers, however, retire every year and the number of elder stocks does not increase. There are many more buyers than there is merchandise in this market. (It might be compared to trying to rent a parking place in one of the best spots in the middle of Tokyo.) The current cost of opening a stable is rumored to be upwards of ¥200 million. This means, of course, that twenty consecutive tournaments as a *juryo* will not produce the necessary funds. Some *rikishi* have actually gone as far as attaining elder status and then having to retire because the money could not be raised.

Obtaining an elder stock does not automatically mean that an elder can open his own stable and start a business. He must first learn how to operate one and then make another tremendous layout of funds to set up housekeeping. In many cases, an elder will remain with his original stable for a while, learning the ropes of the business from his former stablemaster.

How a Small Man Can Get into Sumo

The minimum requirements for passing the new-apprentice examination are a height of 173 cm and weight of 75 kg. Weight can be gained but there is not much that can be done about height. A large number of referees (*gyoji*) and announcers (*yobidashi*) are men who were forced to give up their dreams of becoming *rikishi* because they literally could not measure up. In other words, there are other ways to put that passion for sumo to good use.

There is only one way to become a *rikishi* if the physical requirements cannot be attained. That is to participate in college sumo or sumo for corporate teams. Recently, loopholes have been put into effect to accomodate *rikishi* with exceptional records who do not necessarily meet the standard requirements. It's never too late to take up your loincloth and start stamping! Part of the pleasure of sumo lies in the small getting the better of the large. Strong, small underdogs such as Mainoumi and Kyokudozan make the sport far more interesting.

COMPARING SUMO RANKS
AND POSITIONS IN
A JAPANESE COMPANY

The banzuke ranking system of sumo is unique and somewhat difficult to understand. Comparing it to the positions in a Japanese company, though, should make it clearer.

SUMO	A COMPANY
Scouting activities, fresh arrivals	Reaping the student ranks. The "study trip" offered by the company to the cream of the crop tickles the vanity of the recruits.
New apprentice	The company entrance exam is a mere formality. A few have already set their sights on the president's seat. The world is at their feet.
Sumo Training School	New-employee training. The reality of the company is still unknown.
Jonokuchi "the initial stage"	First assignment. Seniors are cold and superiors glower as you try to get your work done. The pressures of company life force some to change their jobs. "May sickness," the disillusionment that sets in after the first couple of months on the job, is epidemic.

Jonidan
"the second step
of the initial
stage"

In the sumo world, you would be no more than a loincloth carrier. You have been with the company two or three years. You are finally familiar with the job, but your output is still low. Plenty quit at this stage.

Sandanme
"the third step"

You have been with the company five or six years, your job becomes more interesting and you feel the appreciation of your superiors. The seniors that seemed so talented a few years ago no longer induce nearly the same awe.

Makushita
"in front of the
curtain"
It has been
seven years.

You have been given your first position of responsibility, and that means a title under your name on your business card. Your girlfriend is impressed, but your salary is still low.

Juryo
"ten *ryo*" (the
amount of pay
rikishi of this
rank received in
the old days)

At last, you reach duty chief! The others who entered the company with you are still lagging behind. Your position, however, is not comfortable as you feel the pull from behind and the push from above. In sumo, the top *juryo* is known as the god of beggars.

Maegashira
"front of the
head"
levels 10 - 16

Section chief. You are feeling the dignity that accompanies middle management. They're beginning to remember your face at your favorite bars.

Maegashira levels 9 - 4	Assistant division manager. Division manager is just ahead. You find yourself heading for fancy bars on the Ginza for after-hours drinking forays.
Maegashira Levels 3 - 1	Division manager. You've begun to think you may make president after all. Many of your peer group are finding themselves left with no more than dreams of retirement.
Komusubi "the small knot"	General director. At long last, you move into an executive position. Others your age have been moved out of the parent company into positions with lowly affiliates.
Sekiwake "attendant to the barrier"	Managing director. Factional divisions are in constant competition for the president's seat. The opposing faction has spotted you as a central character lurking in the shadows.
Ozeki "the great barrier"	Vice-president. Your goal is right in front of you. You do your work with great efficiency and wait for your chance.
Yokozuna	President. The dream of manhood. The responsibility, however, is tremendous.

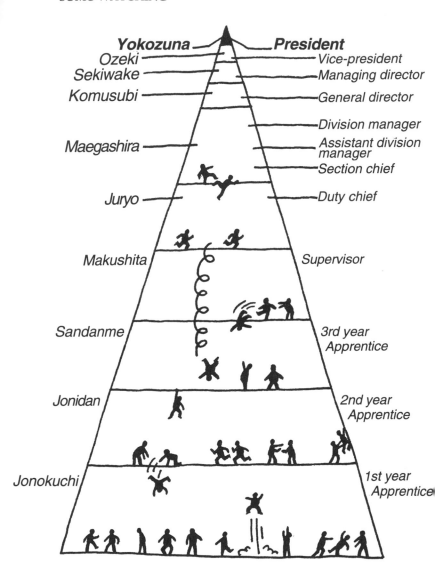

Yokozuna — President
Ozeki — Vice-president
Sekiwake — Managing director
Komusubi — General director
Division manager
Maegashira — Assistant division manager
Section chief
Juryo — Duty chief
Makushita — Supervisor
Sandanme — 3rd year Apprentice
Jonidan — 2nd year Apprentice
Jonokuchi — 1st year Apprentice

How to Read the *Banzuke* Ranking Chart

The *banzuke* chart indicates rankings using different sizes of lettering, once again indicating how rigidly hierarchic the sumo world is. The feelings of the *rikishi* in the bottom ranks are dispensed with for the sake of quick comprehension of who is on top. It is easy to understand the joy and the sorrow of the wrestlers on the list. The *banzuke* is written on thick high grade paper 107 cm x 78 cm in size. It is then reduced to half that size and printed on *washi* paper. The hand-written calligraphy used is unique to the *banzuke* and even called "sumo lettering." Writing up the *banzuke* is the job of the referees. It is done in absolute secrecy after the conclusion of the *banzuke* compilation meeting. It continues to be closely guarded during the printing process to ensure that none of the information leaks out before the official presentation.

Below is an explanation of the *banzuke* printed on p.48. Refer to it while reading the explanations.

1. Sumo has always been divided into east and west teams. From the end of the Meiji era through the first part of the Showa era, tournaments were held as team competitions, with the winners taking possession of the tournament banner. Fans supported not only their favorite *rikishi*, but also their favorite side. In 1947 the team competition was abolished and the tournaments became round-robin events among the different stables. The present east-west division is a mere formality, and bouts are not restricted to east vs. west combinations. A west-side *ozeki* is often named after a place in eastern Japan.

49

1. West   gyoji (referee)   1. East   2.Sei Yokozuna

4. Makushita

3. Juryo

5. Sandanme

6. Jonidan,
   Jonokuchi

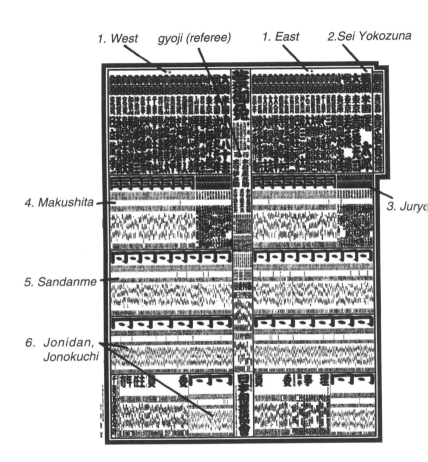

The western *yokozuna* for one tournament may be the eastern *yokozuna* for the next. *Rikishi* do not necessarily remain on one side or the other. Re-compiling the *banzuke* is much the same as a job transfer within the same company. At present there are forty *rikishi* who are of *maegashira* ranking and above who are listed on the top line.

2. The *yokozuna* listed on the top line within the framework are the "regular" *(sei) yokozuna*. Those whose names are written outside the framework arc the "overflow" *(haridashi) yokozuna*. Whether a *yokozuna* is regular or overflow depends on his past win-loss record. Regular *yokozuna* have the better records. Depending on the way the *banzuke* is organized, *ozeki* and *sekiwake* may find themselves listed as "overflow." The east side wrestlers have better records than those on the west. This means that even if two wrestlers have the same rank, the one with the better record for the last tournament will be listed on the east side.

3. *Yokozuna* have their names listed in the largest letters. The size becomes smaller as rank descends: *ozeki, sekiwake, komusubi,* and *maegashira*. The names on the second section of the *banzuke* are written under the title of *maegashira*, but the lettering is smaller than those listed above. These *rikishi* are actually of the *juryo* rank, sometimes called *jumaime* (tenth pagers).

4. From *makushita* on, the print becomes more and more difficult to read, and the thick, sumo lettering gets thinner and denser. In its original size it is quite clear, but the whole chart is reduced in size when printed, to the point where the smallest letters are virtually illegible.

5. *Sandanme.* The names of the *rikishis'* home towns

are written as large as the print used for *makushita*, but the names are smaller.

6. *Jonidan, Jonokuchi*. This section is commonly referred to as "the magnifying glass." The names are written in such tiny print that you need a magnifying glass to read it. The reason for this is the large number of names that have to be included in a very small space. Fans never look at these names. If you ever see anyone examining this part of the *banzuke*, you can be sure they are searching for a close relative.

7. The referees are also ranked. Again, the ranks are indicated by the size of the print, but, because there are only a small number of referees and just enough extra space, the names of the *jonokuchi* referees are printed larger than the names of the *jonokuchi* wrestlers themselves.

Three Ways to Obtain a *Banzuke*

1. Buy one at the Kokugikan Hall. As soon as the *banzuke* for the next tournament has been announced, copies are distributed for ¥50. They usually sell out within a week.

2. Buy one at one of the souvenir booths or tea shops in the hall where the tournament is being held. This is

risky, however, as they may choose not to sell one to you if they are busy or only have a few copies.

3. The support group route. Most stables send out *banzuke* to members of their support groups.

If your interest lies only in the newest rankings, all sports newspapers carry the details the day after they are announced.

Sumo Salaries

The fact that *rikishi* do not receive salaries until they achieve the *juryo* rank is one of the harsher realities of sumo. As soon as they make *sekitori* status, however, the *rikishi* receive salaries that far exceed the standards of those earned by businessmen of the same age. (Even those *makushita* rank and under are paid a small amount. They receive an allowance of ¥60,000 - 80,000 per tournament, and an incentive pay based on their win-loss record.) Actual salaries are listed on the next page. In addition, there is a ¥5 million purse for the winner of *makuuchi* tournaments. *Sekitori* are also eligible for severance pay when they retire.

Another bonus is the money *rikishi* earn for public appearances. It is rumored that a *yokozuna* is paid as much as ¥1 million to attend a reception or party. This sort of money that comes from sponsor groups cannot be ignored as a part of *rikishi* earnings.

Sekitori (monthly salary)			Elders	
Yokozuna	¥1.8	million	Director	¥ 1.017 million
Ozeki	1.497 million		Auditor	.892 million
Sekiwake,			Committee-	
Komusubi	1.077 million		member	.701 million
Maegashira.	.829 million		Participant	.596 million
Juryo	.654 million		Regular	.550 million

What Do Referees and Announcers Do?

In the sumo world of ratings based on wrestling perfor-mance, the referees and announcers are on pay and pro-motion systems which are similar to those of most Japa-nese companies. No matter how talented he may be, a referee or announcer will not be promoted ahead of one of his seniors. For these men, years of earnest labor pave the road to success.

Now, what exactly do referees and announcers do?

Referees are called *gyoji*. In the old days, Shikimori and Kimura were only two of the several families in-volved in the profession, but now these family lines of *gyoji* no longer exist, and only the names remain.

All *gyoji* (and announcers) arrive at their occupation

by way of the sumo stables. As with the *rikishi*, they are members of the Sumo Association, but each makes his living at his respective stable. Between tournaments, *gyoji* are part of the staff that run the stables. They usually take care of general affairs and also have duties with the Japan Sumo Association.

Besides judging bouts, *gyoji* also introduce the wrestlers, broadcast the winning moves, and record the *banzuke* and matches for each bout. In short, sumo *gyoji* are businessmen, judges, announcers, and designers.

As for the *sekitori* they are given *shikona* (wrestling-names) by their *Oyakata* based on either a Chinese character from the *Oyakata's* name, the names of the stables' previous wrestlers or, like Terao, they keep their original name.

All *gyoji* have one of two last names: Shikimori or Kimura. The top-ranked referees "*tate-gyoji*" can be recognized merely by their names: Kimura Shonosuke and Shikimori Inosuke. These top referees are called *Oyakata* by those around them, a title of respect usually awarded only to retired wrestlers.

Of the two *tate-gyoji*, Kimura Shonosuke has the higher rank. Kimura Shonosuke always referees the final bout of the day. When Kimura Shonosuke retires, Shikimori Inosuke is renamed Kimura Shonosuke. It is a unique and complicated system, and to the layman, possibly confusing.

Next, we have the announcers (*yobidashi*). The *tattsuke bakama* (baggy-legged trousers that taper from the knee to the ankle) look very elegant. Nothing is more impressive than the announcer when he spreads his fan and calls out "*Higa-a-shi!*" (On the east...). The announcers do not have special family names. They are usually referred to as Yobidashi So-and-so, meaning that "announcer" is more or less their family name.

Like the *gyoji*, the announcers are in charge of various duties at their stables. They may act as assistants to the stablemaster, receive guests, take telephone calls, and so on. Both *gyoji* and announcers take their meals with *rikishi* who have ranks comparable to their own.

The formal duties of announcers are not limited to calling out the names of *rikishi*. They are in charge of beating the drums inside and outside of the hall to signify the opening of a tournament. They carry banners announcing special prize money offered by outside sources for a bout. Announcers offer "strength-giving water" to *rikishi* whose side has lost the previous bout (it is considered bad luck to receive this water from a losing team mate, therefore only the *rikishi* who win can offer water to the next *rikishi* on his side.) Announcers are also responsible for the constant sweeping outside of the ring between bouts. They are busy people indeed.

The announcers, in fact, make the ring. It takes all thirty-odd announcers three to four days to make the ring before a tournament. Matches held out-of-town between regularly scheduled tournaments require rings for only a day. In these cases, a few announcers get together and do a rush job, piling up beer cases to form its base.

The names of the announcers are not listed on the *banzuke* along with those of *rikishi* and *gyoji*. They were listed at one point for a period of about ten years, but were eventually cut for lack of space. Now their public exposure is limited to live TV broadcasts, keeping them almost totally behind the scenes.

Speaking of behind-the-scenes, there is one more important job that cannot be overlooked; the hairdresser. This is the person who styles the hair of wrestlers into the *mage* or topknot that is their trademark. A hairdresser trains for seven years before he is considered experienced enough to work alone.

Hairdressers, too, belong to individual stables. Only *rikishi* of *sekitori* status are allowed to have the hair at the back of their heads styled into a fan-like shape called "the big gingko leaf" (*oitcho*). Top hairdressers study the hair of each *sekitori*, styling it into the *oitcho* which suits it best. By the way, Hawaiian wrestlers Konishiki and Akebono have their hair straightened before styling.

In short, on the top of the head of every accomplished *rikishi* is a very smart topknot. The *mage* itself lends us a view of this important backstage job.

Ranking *Rikishi* Based on Appearance

Novice sumo fans cannot always put the names of wrestlers together with their faces. They are all big and tall, and it is not easy to tell them apart. Besides the *sekitori rikishi*, there are a great number in the *makushita* rankings. Even if you can't tell them apart individually, there is a way to figure out their ranks:

Wrestlers

1. *Mage* (Topknots)

The hair of the new apprentices is not long enough for a topknot. *Rikishi* with long, unkempt hair are brand new. As soon as it is long enough (it takes about a year) they start wearing their hair in a topknot.

Not until they reach *juryo* are *rikishi* allowed to have their hair styled into the "big gingko leaf." *Makushita* rank and below merely tie their hair up into what is known as a simple *chonmage*. Even for *sekitori*, the fancy styles are reserved for tournament bouts. On days off, they usually tie their hair into a plain *chonmage*.

2. Clothing

Rikishi are often seen in cotton *kimono (yukata)*. *Jonokuchi* and *Jonidan* wrestlers are restricted to this thin layer of clothing all year round. No matter how cold it is, they are bound by a custom that forbids mufflers or coats. If you see a wrestler dressed in a *yukata* in the middle of winter, give him an encouraging word.

Sekitori usually make their entrance at tournaments in a somewhat more formal cotton *kimono* called a *kinagashi*. *Sandanme* are allowed to wear a loose-fitting jacket *(haori)*, but only *sekitori* can wear the *hakama* trousers.

3. *Obi*

Sandanme rikishi and below wear sashes made of a cheap crepe. *Makushita* are allowed to wear *hakata obi* of a somewhat better quality. *Yokozuna* wear genuine crepe sashes with a substantially higher price tag. The higher the rank, the more expensive and tasteful the clothing looks. Rumor has it that all of Konishiki's clothing—from his *yukata* to his loincloth is ordered specially from Sailor's, a popular clothing store for teenagers in Tokyo.

always wears
a *yukata*
(cotton
kimono)

loose hair

Chonmage
topknot

semi-formal
cotton;
kimono may
wear a *haori*
jacket in
formal situa-
tions (from
sandanme)

hakata
sash

cheap
crepe
sash

wooden
geta

New Apprentice

setta (from
sandanme)

Makushita

hair styled into the "big gingko leaf"

hakama trousers (all *sekitori*)

genuine woven-bamboo *setta*

Yokozuna in Formal Dress

4. Footwear

Here, too, *banzuke* ratings are in evidence. *Jonokuchi* and *jonidan* wear wooden *geta* year round. There is no affection in sumo for that clip-clop sound which others may romanticize. Young hopefuls want to escape that hollow echo as soon as possible. *Sandanme* are allowed to wear *setta* (flat sandals). Even here there are ranks. Genuine *setta* made with thin strips of woven bamboo can only be worn by sekitori. The *rikishi* himself is a walking illustration of his position on the ruthless *banzuke*.

Mawashi (loincloth)

This is also called a *shimekomi* (bundle up). The tournament *mawashi* of a *sekitori* is satin. Designated colors of the Sumo Association are black, navy blue, and purple. There are, however, many *rikishi* who prefer brighter colors. Some even appear in the ring in silver or gold. The length of the *mawashi* is usually nine meters (Konishiki's is thirteen meters!)

Rikishi drape firmly starched *sagari* strings from the front of the their *mawashi*. During training sessions, though, *sekitori* wear simple, white cotton *mawashi*.

Makushita rikishi and below have no special satin *mawashi* for tournaments. They wear their cotton training *mawashi*. Their *sagari* are also made of cotton and are inelegant. Colors are restricted to black and purple; white is forbidden for lower ranks.

By the way, *rikishi* are forbidden to wear anything under their *mawashi*. Washing is said to hasten deterioration, so they are only aired out. Cleaning of any form is confined to a little hand scrubbing. *Mawashi* last about a year before they have to be replaced.

Gyoji (Referees)

Referees can also be classified by their appearance. Observation of these elements surrounding sumo makes the sport even more interesting.

Makushita Gyoji

Short trousers

Green or black
tassels

Barefoot,
of course

1. Tassels

The color of the tassels on a *gyoji's* chest, sleeves, and fan denotes his rank. There is even a rank denotation between the two top *gyoji (tate-gyoji)*. Kimura Shonosuke

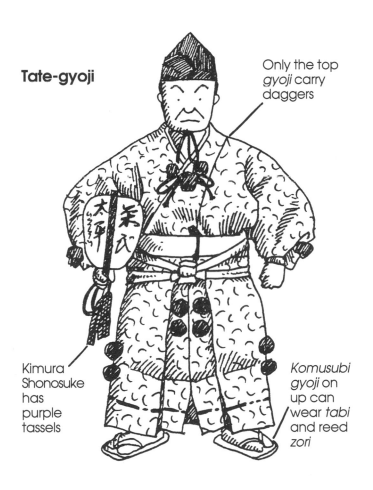

Tate-gyoji

Only the top *gyoji* carry daggers

Kimura Shonosuke has purple tassels

Komusubi gyoji on up can wear *tabi* and reed *zori*

has purple tassels, while those of Shikimori Inosuke are purple and white. *Komusubi, sekiwake,* and *ozeki* referees have red tassels. *Maegashira* have red and white, *juryo* are green and white, while *makushita* are green or black.

2. Dagger

Only the two *tate-gyoji* carry daggers. This indicates that they are so serious about their job that they are willing to commit ritual suicide *(harakiri)* if they should make a wrong call.

3. Footwear

Gyoji wear footwear according to their rank. *Komusubi* referees on up are allowed to wear *tabi* (split-toe socks) and reed *zori. Maegashira* and *juryo gyoji* wear *tabi* only. *Makushita* on down are barefoot. Clothing, of course, is clearly different for *jonokuchi* and *yokozuna* referees. The hems of the trousers of *Makushita gyoji* come up to their knees. Seeing those *gyoji* in their kneepants running around the ring in bare feet is as much fun as watching the bout itself.

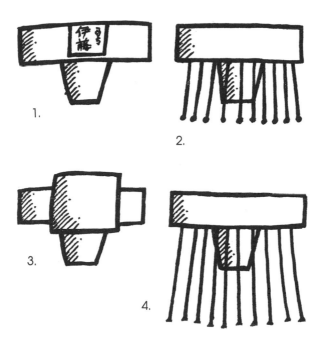

1. *Mawashi* used by new apprentices at the sumo training school. On the front of the black cotton *mawashi* is a piece of white cloth with the name of the *rikishi* and his stable.

2. *Mawashi* used by *makushita* on down. Used during tournaments as well as training. The colors are black or purple. The *sagari* strands are also cotton.

3. *Sekitori* training *mawashi* made of white cotton.

4. *Sekitori* tournament *mawashi*. Both *mawashi* and *sagari* strands are satin. Colors vary and the *sagari* are neatly starched.

Sumo Giants

No matter how you look at them, *rikishi* are big. Deep in the heart of every sumo fan is a childlike amazement that a member of the same human race can grow so big and strong.

These days, quite a few Japanese reach a height of 180 cm, but there are not many who weigh more than 100 kg. As a matter of fact, any sumo wrestler measuring 180 cm will probably weigh 150 kg.

Konishiki is the heaviest *rikishi* in sumo history, tipping the scales at 253.5 kg. He literally squeezes himself into a taxi, reminding one of fitting a model ship into a bottle.

During the Edo era, there were a number of *rikishi* who had heights of 2 m. At present, Akebono is the tallest at 204 cm. I saw him once on the subway, and the guy really is gigantic.

Listed below are the four tallest and five heaviest *rikishi* in the history of sumo.

TALLEST

1. Ikezuki Geitazaemon (Tempo era 1830-1844) **229 cm**

2. Ozora Shikizaemon (Bunsei era 1818-1830) **228 cm**

3. Ryumon Kogoro (Bunsei era 1818-1830) **226 cm**

4. Shakagatake
Kumoemon (Meiwa era 1764-1771) **223 cm**

HEAVIEST

1. Konishiki Yasokichi **264 kg**
2. Hidenoumi Wataru **229 kg**
3. Akebono Taro **212 kg**
4. Onokuni Yasushi **211 kg**
5. Takamiyama Daigoro **205 kg**
   (current Azumazeki *Oyakata*)

Vital Statistics for *Yokozuna* Akebono

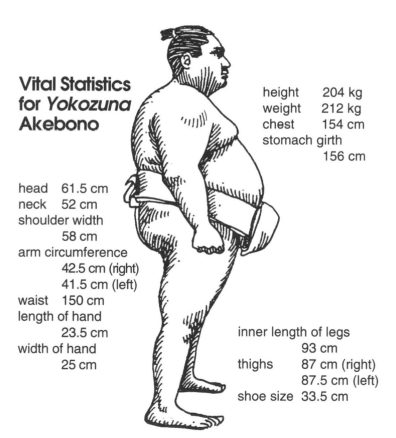

height   204 kg
weight   212 kg
chest   154 cm
stomach girth
            156 cm

head   61.5 cm
neck   52 cm
shoulder width
        58 cm
arm circumference
        42.5 cm (right)
        41.5 cm (left)
waist   150 cm
length of hand
        23.5 cm
width of hand
        25 cm

inner length of legs
            93 cm
thighs   87 cm (right)
            87.5 cm (left)
shoe size   33.5 cm

Average Height and Weight for *Makuuchi Rikishi*

> height: 186 cm (at the 1991 Nagoya Tournament)
> weight: 150.26 kg (at the 1991 Autumn Tournament)

The biggest and the smallest *rikishi*

(at the 1991 Nagoya Tournament)

height: Akebono 204 cm

Mainoumi 174 cm

(official height; actual height is 171 cm)
> (He managed to pass his height test because of the
> silicone transplant mentioned previously.)

—a difference of 30 (or 33) cm.

weight: Konishiki 253.5 kg

Mainoumi 94.5 kg

—a difference of 159 kg.

A Record of Takanohana (Takahanada)'s Growth

Spring 1988
First tournament
Juryo
height 182 cm
weight 121 kg

September 1989
Juryo

height 184 cm
weight 110 kg

Summer 1990
Maegashira

height 184 cm
weight 121 kg

Why *Rikishi* Get Fat

There are not too many athletes who actually work at gaining weight. Why is it preferable to be bigger in the world of sumo? This has a great deal to do with the ring.

The ring has a diameter of 455 cm. When a bout begins, there is only 70 cm between the two wrestlers. More than speed, impact is important. In order to put power into that first instant of impact, speed and power are important, but putting weight behind that speed is an even greater weapon. *Rikishi* also use their weight to absorb the impact of their opponents.

Of course, it is important to gain weight in a balanced fashion. Takanohana (the former Takahanada) is one good example of this. His burgeoning talent has shone through at each stage of his growth. Chiyonofuji (now Kokonoe *Oyakata*) began to gain weight when he quit smoking, at which point he also gained an impressive amount of strength and began his surge towards *yokozuna* status.

Nagoya 1991
Komusubi
height 186 cm
weight 133 kg

Winter 1992
Sekiwake
height 186 cm
weight 130 kg

Spring 1993
Ozeki
height 185 cm
weight 142 kg

A wrestler's lifestyle greatly influences his weight gain. He wakes up early, 4 or 5 a.m., and trains vigorously for several hours, cleans the practice ring, and then sits down for an enormous meal after which he takes a well-earned nap.

Rikishi eat only two meals a day, and experience has taught that food is absorbed better this way.

Middle-aged Businessmen Have More Fat!

You might be saying to yourself, "OK, so they're strong, but who wants to be that fat?" In fact, you might be the one with the excess fat.

There are lots of *rikishi* with a good layer of fat on them, but under that are hidden muscles to rival Hercules. You may think that your stomach is no more than a modest paunch, but how much muscle do you have? According to one survey, a businessman 172 cm tall and weighing 75 kg has a higher percentage of fat than a chunky wrestler 178 cm tall, weighing 138 kg. In other words, the businessman is the one who is overweight. Businessmen do not get enough exercise, so they become overweight as their muscles weaken, even though their appearance may not change. In other words, sumo wrestlers are not necessarily those with the excess fat problem.

In his prime, the popular *yokozuna* Chiyonofuji had 11% body fat. The average rate for men in their 20s is 13%, meaning Chiyonofuji was below average. *Rikishi* have extra bodyweight, but they also have muscle. They are not suffering from middle-age spread.

Anglers and Soup

In the sumo world, chunky *rikishi* are called *anko* and thinner wrestlers are *soppu*.

**Anko-
type
wrestler**

**Soppu-
type
wrestler**

Both of these words come from *chanko-nabe*, the one-pot stew that *rikishi* eat. *Anko* means "angler," the name of the fish in the stew. It is plump and has a round stomach. *Soppu* was originally "soup"—the broth of the stew, and conjures up a vision of the chicken carcass used for stock.

Legends of Supernatural Strength

There are lots of stories about the supernatural strength of *rikishi*.

One famous story has to do with the visit of Commodore Matthew C. Perry to Japan in his "black ships." The shogunate were awed and slightly intimidated by the differences in strength between Japan and the United States. When the merchants requested that a sumo exhibition be held for the fleet, the shogunate realized that this would be a good chance to show off one of the few strengths of the Japanese and quickly agreed to the plan. Preceding the exhibition, the *ozeki* Koyanagi and thirty others climbed onto the ships bearing gifts of rice in 50 kg sacks. While the sailors could not lift even one sack, the *rikishi* carried two or three each.

One of the wrestlers, Shiramayumi, outdid the rest. He carried eight sacks. Four on his back, two tied to his chest, and one in each hand. The main event was a bout between Koyanagi and three sailors. The sailors were all known for their boxing or wrestling prowess, but Koyanagi managed to beat them all effortlessly. At any rate, the shogunate succeeded in astounding the Americans.

The first Wakanohana (retired Futagoyama *Oyakata*, uncle of Takanohana and Wakanohana) once carried four 18-liter kegs of sake on his head. One Iwamatsu, a member of the Wakamatsu stable, is said to have effortlessly shouldered a 25-meter length of railroad steel. Tachiyama, a *yokozuna* of the Taisho era, once carried a 500 kg-cannonball without breaking into a sweat. These are but a few examples of incredible feats of sumo strength!

An Impact of 800 kg

The power behind the first moment of impact greatly influences the outcome of a bout. This impact is determined by the burst of strength and by sheer weight. If two *rikishi* are the same weight, the advantage goes to the *rikishi* with the greatest speed. If they are equally matched in speed, the advantage goes with whoever is heaviest. Kitanoumi (now Kitanoumi *Oyakata*) has the greatest recorded balance of speed and weight, with an impact of 800 kg.

Grip is also a key element. At present, Konishiki and Akebono have the strongest grips. Their right hands are capable of 90 kg and their left hands of 91 kg. The *makuuchi* average is 75 kg (right hand). The average adult male has a grip of 40-50 kg. This means that the average wrestler is 1.5 times stronger than average, with Konishiki's grip twice as strong. Chiyonofuji also had a powerful grip, recording 100+ kg. This was said to be how he compensated for his smaller size. A sumo wrestler with a strong grip is said to be capable of crushing an apple with his bare hand. A real human juicer!

Eating is Part of the Job

Rikishi eat! The first requirement for a strong body is food. Next comes training. A sumo stable is an eating heaven where second helpings are unlimited.

During the Edo era, a stable served as a form of emergency relief, a place for parents to send large youths who they could not afford to feed. It was not long ago that one of the main motivations for joining a stable was merely the fact that there was never a shortage of food.

Tales of eating and drinking also add to the superhuman aura of *rikishi*. In the old days, sponsors used to enjoy just watching their favorite wrestlers eat and drink.

Big Equipment for Big Men

There are some things that we take for granted in everyday life that are thoroughly impractical for big people. *Rikishi* shop at stores that specialize in large items or have things made to order. Sumo *geta* have to be made from the hardest pieces of paulownia wood, and the

74

blocks attached to the soles are extra thick. *Tabi* (split-toe socks) have specially reinforced soles.

The toilet for wrestlers at the new Kokugikan Hall is 1.5 times the normal size. This jumbo toilet was developed especially for *rikishi*. The height is 25 cm, the length of the seat is 58 cm, and the width is 50 cm. The drainage hole is large, too. This is only natural considering the amount of food wrestlers eat. There are many inconveniences for people so big!

Drink Like a Whale, Eat Like a Horse

One of the biggest drinkers in recent history was Nankairyu, a now-retired *rikishi* of Samoan descent. His stablemaster had forbidden him to drink at all, but he happened to come across the store of sake in the stable kitchen. It is said that he started drinking that afternoon and didn't stop till the next night.

Raiden, during the Edo era, drank two 18-liter casks of *sake*. The original Asashio was said to be able to down 36 bottles of beer and six bottles of *sake* in one evening. *Yokozuna* Miyagiyama ate fifteen bowls of eel on rice (*unagi-donburi*). But the eating record goes to *yokozuna* Ozutsu who ate 7.5 kg of sweet potatoes and 36 bowls of rice.

THE RING

The Age of the Square Ring

It was not so long ago, in the long, long history of sumo, that bouts began taking place in a round ring.

During the Edo era, the boundaries were not even clearly defined. The spectators formed a kind of human ring. The aim of sumo was to throw your opponent down onto the ring or out of it into the human fence. The border was very vague and it was impossible to make any close calls accurately. This resulted in quarrels and fights, and, eventually, a ban on the sport.

Pictures from the *Kanmon era* show a ring with four pillars and a borderline made of rope. The pillars look almost like the cornerposts of a boxing ring. During the Edo era, the border was changed from rope to barrels placed around the ring, making it a *dohyo*, or, literally, "dirt and barrels." By the Jokyo era (1684-87), the square ring had become round, and, finally, the barrels were buried in the dirt of the ring.

The Round Ring is What Makes Sumo Interesting

The round ring is a phenomena unique to sumo. It is much more practical than the rings of any other combative sport. The lack of corners allows for smooth footwork and prevents any cornering tactics. It provides for a smoother bout and a higher class of performance. It can even be said that much of the appeal of sumo is a result of the round ring.

There is more to the simple-looking *dohyo* than meets the eye. Let's learn the basics of this bare stage.

Excerpts from Ring Regulations

1. The height of the *dohyo* is 54-60 cm, with a square circumference of 6 m 70 cm. The dirt is packed down hard and a circle with a diameter of 4 m 55 cm formed on top using barrels.

2. Six-tenths of each barrel is buried in the dirt, with the other four-tenths exposed. Arakida dirt is used to pack the barrels in. Sand is packed down hard so that no footprints will remain when *rikishi* stamp.

3. Twenty barrels define the border line. Sixteen are regular-sized and four are slightly smaller, with one placed slightly outside the ring in each of the four directions.

Toku Barrels

There are four *toku* barrels, one representing each of the four directions. They are placed slightly outside the ring itself. *Toku* means "advantage." The barrels are advantageously placed so that they provide a little extra space for a wrestler backed up to the edge of the ring. The original purpose for these openings was to allow rain water to drain from outdoor rings.

The Quality of the Ring Depends on the Dirt

The ring is made of Arakida dirt that comes from the banks of the Arakawa River in Saitama Prefecture. It has a high clay content, making it perfect for the purpose. This clay, however, has become difficult to come by from its original source, and is now being brought in from Ibaraki Prefecture.

The quality of the ring is 80% dependent upon the dirt. It should not crumble when held nor can it be too sticky. Finding the right kind of dirt for tournaments outside of Tokyo is always a problem. The elder in charge of the ring has to visit the area ahead of time and arrange for the proper dirt.

At the Kokugikan Hall, only the top one-third of the dirt is replaced for each tournament. Even this requires eight tons of soil. As exhibition bouts are only held for a few days, dirt is conserved by using beer crates for the base of the ring.

As mentioned before, making the ring is the job of the announcers. The dirt has to be packed, the ring measured, and the barrels buried. It is a difficult job.

Objects are Buried in the Ring

As wrestlers make their living in the *dohyo*, it is said that "money is buried in the ring." There is a story, of course, of a wrestler who took the saying literally, and was disappointed to find nothing but dirt when he actually dug it up. Actually, there are some things buried in it. The day before the start of an official tournament, a type of christening ceremony is held for the ring, and at the point where the wrestlers will be facing off the next day, six items are buried; some torreya nuts, washed rice, chestnuts, kelp, dried cuttlefish, and salt. (All of these items are either believed to bring good luck or stand for purification.) Finally, the entire ring is purified with salt and *sake*. The purpose of the ceremony is to guard the wrestlers from accidents and ensure their safety.

The Bull's Eye Ring

At the beginning of the Showa era (1926), the ring was shaped like a bull's eye, with a double circle shape. The inside ring was smaller than it is now (3.9 m in diameter), and the space between the two rings, which marked the ring's boundary, was filled in with sand. The purpose of this sand was to indicate which rikishi had stepped outside first. Eventually, the inner circle was abandoned and the ring expanded to the size of the outer circle, 4.55 m in diameter, with sand spread around the outside of that; and thus it remains to the present. This is the sand that the announcers sweep after each bout.

The Ring was Enlarged Again for One Tournament

Prior to the 1946 November Tournament, the rule governing the size of the ring at the Kokugikan Hall was changed to allow for an enlargement to 4.8m. This change in size was made during the confusion following

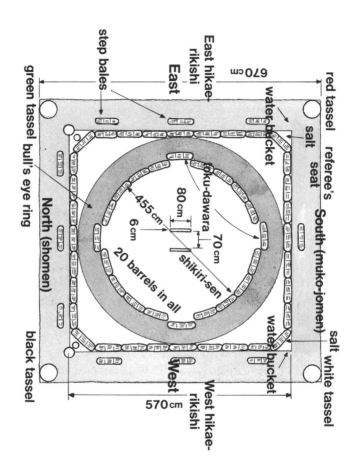

the end of World War II. The purpose was to make sumo more attractive to the occupying forces who had taken over the hall. This change enraged the *rikishi*. One in particular, *yokozuna* Futabayama, sat out the tournament in protest. (He retired during the following tournament, with his disappointment in this change the apparent cause.) However, this change was only temporary, and the ring was returned to its original size for the next tournament.

The Four Directions of the Ring

The ring has an east, west, south, and north side. If you have ever watched sumo on TV, you will have noticed that *rikishi* on the west team are called from their waiting positions on the west side. East team *rikishi* wait on the eastern side. The northern side is called the front, and the south is the "opposite front side." When the announcer calls out "Mr. So-and-so on the opposite front side," he is referring to a reporter on the southern perimeter of the ring.

When you look at the roof over the ring which is strung from the ceiling of the hall, you may notice the tassels hanging from the drape below it. Each of the four tassels are a different color. North (the tassel in the northwest corner) is designated using black. East (the northeast corner) is green. South (the southeast corner) is red, and west (the southwest corner) is white. If the "judge under the black tassel" is mentioned, it is a reference to the elder acting as a judge at the front of the ring. The tassels represent the seasons of the year and their accompanying deities. North is winter, East is spring, South is summer, and West is autumn.

Salt and Strength-giving Water

Ceremonies of salt and water are two elements of sumo that set it apart from other sports.

The ring is a place of competition, but it is also holy ground. This is a special feature of sumo, the highly-spiritual aspect of its combination of sport and religion.

Salt is used not only to purify the ring, but also as an effective disinfectant for cuts. It is said that salt sprinkled on the ring prevents infection of cuts and scrapes to the almost-naked *rikishi*.

It is interesting to notice the different ways salt is tossed around the ring. Some *rikishi* use copious amounts, others only sprinkle a little bit. Some wipe it on their chests, others put it in their mouths. Observing these differences alone can be fun. Because tournaments have to maintain a schedule, however, only *makushita* wrestlers and above are permitted to toss salt. Here, once again, the discriminatory *banzuke* comes into play.

It has been estimated that more than 40 kg of salt is used per day of a tournament. At present there is no limit to the amount that can be tossed. During World War II, however, limits were set because the country had so few resources available. Extravagant use of salt was considered unpatriotic. The current wrestler who uses the largest amounts of salt is Mitoizumi. At the London tournament, he was known to the fans as "The Salt Shaker."

Like salt, water is used for purification, but it also represents determination to fight to the death. A winning *rikishi* offers a drink of strength-giving water to the next *rikishi* on his side, who uses it to rinse out his mouth and then spits it out. (As mentioned before, receiving the water from a losing wrestler is considered unlucky, so an announcer offers it in his place.)

When a bout goes on for too long, and no decision can be reached, the *gyoji* will call a halt (literally "water is added") and the *rikishi* take another drink of water before resuming their fight.

Chirichozu

When a *rikishi* is called into the ring, he stamps twice, receives the water, and takes his place at a *toku* barrel. He then squats down (a position called *sonkyo*), and puts his arms out in front of him. He claps his hands once and then spreads his arms out to his side, turning his palms up. This is called the *chirichozu* ceremony. It appears to be a remnant from the age of outdoor sumo, when water was not used for purification. A *rikishi* pulled up some grass and then rubbed it between his hands to purify his body. By spreading out his arms, the *rikishi* showed his opponent that he was not carrying any weapons. There are certain religious meanings associated with the ceremony as well, but I didn't want to dwell on complicated explanations.

The Fight Begins

After the *chirichozu* ceremony, the *rikishi* stamp their feet again and toss some salt. They then take their marks.

The *gyoji* gives no sign, nor does he blow a whistle. The opposing wrestlers synchronize their breathing, meet each other's eyes, and dash. Thus the bout begins. An instant of difference in this delicate timing influences a bout tremendously. A wrestler can easily lose because of a millisecond delay.

Many people are put off by the time it takes to get a bout started. To them it is boring, but to the *rikishi* themselves, it is the tensest part of the entire bout. Put yourselves in their place for a different perspective on the matter.

"Mat-ta!"

If two *rikishi* miscalculate each other's signals and one rushes the other too quickly, one can call *"Mat-ta,"* (literally "Wait!") and have the bout replayed.

The Japan Sumo Association has made it clear to

rikishi that this tactic must not be used with any frequency because it detracts from the overall image of the sport. The fans give each bout their strictest attention, and if the tension in the air is broken too often, they will lose interest.

Originally, there was no time limit to the preliminary stage of a bout. It could go on for ten or twenty minutes, holding up the tournament interminably. Eventually a time limit was set.

Makuuchi bouts are allowed four minutes from the time the wrestlers are called into the ring until the initial charge is made. When the *gyoji* calls out *"Mat-ta nashi!"* (No more waiting,) the *rikishi* have to charge after placing their fists on the ground of the ring. When the *gyoji* makes this final call, the fans become agitated as they anticipate the beginning of the action. As of the 1991 Autumn Tournament, wrestlers are liable for calling *"matta"* after the set time limit. *Makuuchi rikishi* are fined ¥100,000 and *juryo rikishi* ¥50,000.

"Hakkeyoi" and *"Nokotta"*

The instant two *rikishi* charge, the *gyoji* begins calling out *"Nokotta! Nokotta!"* This is a term which implies, "Who will be left standing?" When they are in a clinch, neither able to move, the *gyoji* calls out *"Hakkeyoi!"* or *"Yoi, hakkeyoi!"* He is encouraging the *rikishi* to try harder. In other words, *nokotta* is used while the wrestlers are in motion, and *hakkeyoi* is meant to goad them out of an immobile state.

Mono-ii

Judges, elders in the Japan Sumo Association, sit around the ring and declare that they have "something to say" or *mono-ii* if they disagree with a *gyoji*'s call. The head judge confers with the elder in the video room using an earphone. If they decide that the two *rikishi* went down simultaneously, they call for a rematch. If they overturn the decision of the referee in the ring, it is called a "difference with the *gyoji*."

A rematch is a tournament "freebie." The *rikishi* have already spent their strength, so a rematch is not easy for them, but it adds an element of change to the day's program for the spectators.

A *gyoji* whose decisions are overturned too often may be demoted. His promotion, therefore, is based on his lack of negative results.

WATCHING
SUMO ON TV

There are More Than 48 Moves

After you have learned how a bout works, the next step is to learn the individual moves. Consider yourself an official sumo fan if you can call the winning move. Give your prowess further marks if you can announce the winning move before the TV broadcaster does.

Sumo moves are referred to collectively as *shijuhatte,* literally "forty-eight hands." There used to be exactly forty-eight moves: twelve throws, twelve trips, twelve backward pulls, and twelve twists. Now the term *shijuhatte* is only an adjective that means "a great number." The actual number of moves has increased, and was officially set at seventy in 1960. Many of the moves are no more than subtle variations on others, making it actually quite difficult for amateurs to recognize them.

Because of the slight differences, some moves are hardly ever formally announced. For example, the *maki-otoshi* is very similar to the *tsuki-otoshi* but you will rarely ever hear a call for the former, as a *maki-otoshi* is usually called as a *tsuki-otoshi*, a very common move. Some moves are so difficult that they are rarely attempted during a tournament.

It is difficult for broadcasters and the judges positioned outside the ring to make precise calls. Listening to retired *rikishi* who often assist broadcasters, you will frequently find them giving results which differ from the official outcome.

THE 70 MOVES: EXPLANATION AND DIFFICULTY LEVEL

***** A highly unusual move seen about once every ten years
**** An uncommon move you may be able to see once every few years
*** A move seen once a year or so
** A move made several times per tournament
* A popular move made daily at any tournament

---

1. *Tsuki-dashi* **
   Thrust out
   > Immediately after standing up to fight, the *rikishi* forcefully thrusts his opponent out of the ring without grasping his belt.

2. *Tsuki-taoshi* ***
   Thrust down
   > Same as *tsuki-dashi*, except that the opponent falls down on or outside the ring.

3. *Oshi-dashi* *
   Frontal push-out
   > Similar to *tsuki-dashi*. The *rikishi* pushes his opponent in the side, chest or throat until he steps over the edge of the ring.

4. *Oshi-taoshi* *
   Frontal push-down
   > Same as *oshi-dashi*, except that the opponent falls.

5. *Yori-kiri* *
   Frontal force-out

Tsuki-dashi

Most common winning move. While the *rikishi* are
in a clinch, one forces the other out of the ring.

6. *Yori-taoshi* *

   Frontal crush-out

   Feat of strength similar to *yori-kiri*. The *rikishi* floors
   his opponent outside the ring.

7. *Abise-taoshi* *

   Backward force-down

   In the *yori-kiri* position, the *rikishi* forces his opponent to fall inside the ring.

8. *Shitate-nage* *

   Under-arm throw

   The *rikishi* throws his opponent down by passing
   his arms over his opponent's arms in a cross-grip
   hold and grabbing his belt.

9. *Uwate-nage* *

   Over-arm throw

   The *rikishi* throws his opponent down, grasping his
   belt by passing his arms over his opponent's arms.

Oshi-dashi

10. *Kote-nage* *
    Arm-lock throw

    The *rikishi* locks his opponent's arms and throws him by vigorously shaking and squeezing the locked arms.

11. *Sukui-nage* *

    The *rikishi* passes his arms under the arms of his opponent and throws the opponent without grasping his belt by scooping up his upper body.

12. *Uwate-dashi-nage* **
    Outer arm throw

    A kind of *uwate-nage*. The *rikishi* throws his opponent down by pulling him.

13. *Shitate-dashi-nage* **
    Inner arm throw

    The *rikishi* passes his arms under those of his opponent and pulls him down. The *rikishi* grasps the front part of his belt when making the throw.

Yori-kiri

14. *Koshi-nage* *****
    Hip-lift throw

    > The *rikishi* pulls his opponent's body tightly and throws him by bouncing him off his hip.

15. *Kubi-nage* **
    Head-lock throw

    > The *rikishi* throws his opponent down by putting his arm around the other's neck.

16. *Ippon-zeoi* *****
    Over-the-shoulder throw

    > Similar to a judo shoulder throw technique. The *rikishi* holds his opponent by the wrist and throws him over his shoulder.

17. *Nicho-nage* ***
    Leg-sweep throw

    > The *rikishi* throws his opponent by tripping his pivot foot. A similar judo technique is called *haraigoshi*.

Kote-nage

18. *Yagura-nage* ****
    Pendulum throw
    > The *rikishi* pulls his opponent closely with one foot pressing against the thigh of his opponent, then throws him by lifting and swinging his body on this foot.

19. *Kake-nage* **
    Arm-leg combined throw
    > The *rikishi* throws down his opponent by putting his foot between the other's legs. A similar judo technique is called *uchimata*.

20. *Tsukami-nage* *****
    Lift throw
    > Grasping the back of his opponent's belt, the *rikishi* throws him as he might a big bag of rice.

21. *Uchi-gake* **
    Inner-leg trip
    > A foot move of tripping the opponent by putting one foot between his legs.

Uwate-nage

22. *Soto-gake* **
    Outer leg trip
    The *rikishi* throws down his opponent by hooking his leg from the outside and leaning heavily on him.

23. *Chon-gake* ***
    Heel-brace force-down
    The *rikishi* trips his opponent by pressing the other's ankle with his own.

24. *Kiri-kaeshi* **
    Twisting backward knee trip
    Counterthrust. Preventing himself from being thrown, the *rikishi* braces his feet and throws his opponent backwards or sideways.

25. *Kawazu-gake* ***
    Backward lift-counter trip
    When the *rikishi* stand side by side, one throws the other backward by putting his foot around that of the other and holding him by the neck.

Shitate-nage

26. *Ke-kaeshi* ***
    Footsweep
    > The *rikishi* slaps his opponent while at the same time kicking his pivot foot.

27. *Ketaguri* ***
    Inside ankle-kick pull down
    > A kind of footsweep. The *rikishi* pulls his opponent down by pulling his hand.

28. *Mitokoro-zeme* ****
    Triple attack force-out
    > Forcing out by simultaneously attacking three parts of the body. For example, a *rikishi* forces his opponent out by locking his feet and pressing his head against the other's chest.

29. *Watashi-komi* ***
    Thigh-grabbing push-down
    > Grabbing his opponent's knee with one hand, the *rikishi* pushes his opponent's body down with the other hand.

30. *Nimai-geri* ****
    Ankle-lick twist-down

Uchi-gake

When his opponent puts his weight on his feet to resist lifting, the *rikishi* twists his body down by sweeping his feet.

31. *Komata-sukui* ***

Over-thigh scoop dump

When his opponent braces his feet in an open stance to resist a pulling throw, the *rikishi* scoops up the other's closest inside thigh.

32. *Soto-komata* ****

Under-thigh scoop dump

Similar to *komata-sukui*. The *rikishi* grabs his opponent's outer thigh.

33. *Oomata* *****

Open-stance thigh-grabbing dump

The *rikishi* grabs his opponent's foot which is farthest away from him and scoops it up .

34. *Tsuma-tori* ****

Leg-lift dump

The *rikishi* moves swiftly to the back of his opponent and grabs his ankle to trip him face down.

Soto-gake

35. *Ashi-tori* ****

    Two-handed leg tip-over

    Throwing an opponent by grabbing his feet with both hands.

36. *Suso-tori* ***

    Ankle-grabbing backward dump

    When his opponent loses his balance, the *rikishi* grabs his nearest leg close to the ankle and dumps him by pressing himself tightly against the other's body.

37. *Suso-harai* ***

    Backward footsweep

    When his opponent turns himself sideways, the *rikishi* forcefully sweeps his feet.

38. *Izori* ****

    Submarine scoop reverse dump

    When his opponent leans forward, the *rikishi* holds the other's body in a half squat and throws him backward by bouncing him off his own body.

39. *Tasuki-zori* ****

    Shoulder sacrifice throw.

Shumoku-zori

A sort of sideways *izori*. The *rikishi* holds his opponent sideways and throws him down.

40. *Shumoku-zori* *****
    Bell hammer shoulder throw
    A rough move similar to a judo technique. The *rikishi* brings his opponent's body high up on his shoulder and dumps him.

41. *Soto-tasuki-zori* *****
    Cat-fooling throw
    Without using the neck or shoulder, the *rikishi* pushes his opponent down by grabbing his arm and inner thigh.

42. *Kake-zori* *****
    Leg-kick sacrifice throw
    A type of *izori*. The *rikishi* throws his opponent sideways by hooking his leg from the outside and leaning heavily on him.

43. *Tsuki-otoshi* *
    Thrust down
    When his opponent pushes forcefully, the *rikishi*

Kubi-nage

jerks his body away and dumps the other on the ring by pushing him by the arm or shoulder joint.

44. *Maki-otoshi* ***

Sideways twist throw

Without grabbing the belt, the *rikishi* twists his opponent by putting one arm around his back and throwing him down with the other arm.

45. *Tottari* **

Arm-bar throw

A move in which the *rikishi* pulls his opponent's hand and throws him over himself.

46. *Saka-tottari* **

Arm-bar counter throw

A kind of *tottari*. A *rikishi* pulls his opponent's hand from the back and throws him face down.

47. *Kata-sukashi* **

Under-shoulder swing down

When his opponent thrusts out his arm, the *rikishi* scoops it up and throws him down, holding him by the shoulder joint.

48. *Soto-musou* ***
    Outer-thigh-grabbing twist-down
    > In a cross-hold grip, the *rikishi* pulls back his arm to grab his opponent's knee and pushes him down by pulling the other arm.

49. *Uchi-musou* ***
    Inner-thigh-grabbing twist-down
    > Similar to the move above, except that in this move, the *rikishi* throws his opponent down by scooping up the inside of his knee.

50. *Zubu-neri* ****
    Elbow-twist throw
    > Holding his opponent by the shoulder, the *rikishi* presses his head against the other's neck and twists him down.

51. *Uwate-hineri* **
    Twisting over-arm throw
    > The *rikishi* throws down his opponent by reaching over his arms to grab his belt and twist him down.

52. *Shitate-hineri* **
    Twisting under-arm throw
    > Throwing down an opponent by grabbing his belt under his arms and twisting him down. The *rikishi* can use momentum by throwing his opponent first and then twisting him down.

53. *Ami-uchi* *****
    Net-casting twist-down
    > Pushed to the edge of the ring, the *rikishi* holds his opponent's arms with both of his own and twists him in a sacrifice throw. The move looks as if the *rikishi* is casting a net.

Hikkake

54. *Saba-ori* ****

   Forward force-down

   > A feat of strength. The *rikishi* forces his opponent
   > down on his knees by pulling his belt forward
   > with his jaw pressed against the other's shoulder.

55. *Harima-nage* ****

   Rear-belt throw

   > A sacrifice move. The *rikishi* grabs the back of his
   > opponent's belt and throws him down at the
   > edge of the ring.

56. *Hikkake* ***

   Arm-grabbing force-out

   > The *rikishi* turns himself slightly sideways to
   > dodge his opponent's thrust-out arm so that the
   > opponent is driven out of the ring by his own mo-
   > mentum.

Hataki-komi

57. *Hataki-komi* *

    Hand pull-down

    > At the moment the *rikishi* stand up to fight, one brings down the other by slapping his low-placed shoulder or back.

58. *Kaina-hineri* ***

    Two-handed arm twist-down

    > A *rikishi* throws down his opponent by grabbing his arm with both hands and twisting it outward. His opponent's body moves in a direction opposite to that of the *tottari*.

59. *Gassho-hineri* ****

    Clasped-hands twist throw

    > A *rikishi* puts both of his hands in a clasped position at the back of his opponent's neck and twists him down.

Tsuri-dashi

60. *Tsuri-dashi* *

    Lift-out

    > A move which entails carrying the opponent outside of the ring by grabbing his belt and lifting him out.

61. *Tsuri-otoshi* **

    Lift dump

    > A feat of strength. The *rikishi* lifts his opponent up and dumps him outside the ring.

62. *Kubi-hineri* ****

    Twisting head throw

    > Twisting an opponent by holding by the neck with one hand and grabbing his arm with the other.

63. *Hiki-otoshi* *

    Hand pull-down

    > A *rikishi* pulls down his opponent by dodging the other's thrust-out arm and jerking his own body away.

64. *Okuri-dashi* *
    Rear push-out
    > The *rikishi* pushes his opponent from behind, making use of the other's own force.

65. *Okuri-taoshi* **
    Rear push-down
    > Same as *okuri-dashi*, except that the opponent falls.

66. *Wari-dashi* ***
    Upper-arm force-out
    > A feat of strength. The *rikishi* pushes his opponent by the upper arm at the edge of the ring until he steps out.

67. *Utchari* *
    Backward pivot throw (Throw down at edge of ring)
    > A sacrifice move used when the *rikishi* is driven to the edge of the ring. He leans backwards carrying his opponent over him and out of the ring.

68. *Kime-dashi* ***
    Elbow-clamp force-out
    > A *rikishi* clamps down on his opponent's arms, which are grasping his own belt, at the elbows and forces him out of the ring.

69. *Kime-taoshi* ***
    Elbow-clamp force-down
    > Same as *kime-dashi*, except that the opponent falls.

70. *Yobi-modoshi* ****
    Backward push-down
    > A rough move. In a cross-hold grip, the *rikishi* gives his opponent a strong pull. At the moment the other's body is lifted up, the wrestler twists him downward.

Other Techniques and Moves

There are eight moves which are forbidden in sumo. A *rikishi* who breaks the rules loses automatically. They are often demonstrated in an amusing manner as an attraction called *shokkiri*, a part of *Hana-zumo* performed at exhibitions commemorating a retiring *rikishi*.

1. Punching with a clenched fist
2. Pulling hair on purpose
3. Stabbing at eyes or other orifices
4. Pulling both ears using both hands simultaneously
5. Grabbing at the vertical strip of the loincloth which covers the genitals
6. Grabbing for the throat
7. Kicking the stomach or chest
8. Bending back one or two fingers

It is a well-known fact that any *rikishi* who loses his loincloth takes an automatic loss (also known as an "unclean loss.")

There are cases where the *rikishi* on the offensive mistakenly steps out of the ring and takes a loss. There is also a "cat-fooling" trick where a *rikishi* claps his hands in front of the face of his opponent and uses the moment of confusion to take the offense. (This was never considered a winning technique until Mainoumi began having success with it.)

Other unusual outcomes include one which happened in 1909. A small wrestler named Tachiyama was completely itimidated by the reputation of his opponent,

Yajimayama. Before they could rush at each other, Yajimayama backed himself right out of the ring. The decision was "win by stare down."

If a *rikishi* incurs a serious injury in the midst of a bout it can be halted and declared a "tie by pain."

Other Sumo Terms

Below are some terms related to techniques other than winning moves. Learning them will make watching sumo even more fun. You'll know you are a real fan when you find these words a normal part of your vocabulary.

Buchikamasu—Beating an opponent's chest with one's own head during the charge.

Kachiageru—Forcing an opponent's lowered head up by jabbing his jaw or chest with one's elbow.

Tsuppari —Hitting an opponent's chest with the palm of one's hand. Doing the same thing to the face is called *harite*.

Nodowa—Hitting an opponent's throat with the palm of one's hand and pushing him back.

Migiyotsu—Thrusting one's right hand between an opponent's arm and side, and grabbing his loincloth.

The same move with the left hand is called *hidariyotsu*). When both have a good hold on each other, it is called *gappuriyotsu*. When neither can get a handle on the other, it is a *namakurayotsu*.

Sashite-arasoi—Fending off one's opponent while trying to get in an advantageous position to grab his loincloth.

Morozashi—Getting both hands at an opponent's side and grabbing his loincloth.

Maemitsu—*Mitsu'* is the loincloth. The front of the loincloth is *maemitsu*. The side is *yokomitsu*. The part that covers the genitals is *tatemitsu*, and it is against the rules to grab it.

Kaina—The arm.

Gaburiyori—Dodging so one's opponent cannot get ahold of you, and then pushing him out of the ring.

Shinitai—A *rikishi* who has obviously had enough even though the match is not yet over. A *rikishi* in no position to fight back.

Kabaite—When both *rikishi* fall at the same time, and the hand of the one on top hits the dirt first. If that *rikishi* has had the clear advantage, he will not take the loss.

Isamiashi—Dragging one's opponent to the edge of the ring and mistakenly stepping out of the ring first. This is a loss.

Sumo Slang

Sumo has its own slang. They are probably meant for the exclusive use of *rikishi*, but some have already entered mainstream usage. Many have funny nuances. Try out a few for fun!

Ika o kimeru (Make like a squid)
> A squid gives out a burst of black ink when it makes its escape, hence this term means to run off after raking in the winnings.
>
> "We were all playing poker last when he made like a squid."

Kao ja nai (That's not in his face)
> To presume to be tougher or more talented than one really is.
>
> "Did you know he's being promoted?"
>
> "Promoted? That's not in his face."

Gachinko (Crash bang)
> To face a challenge head on.
>
> "My date tomorrow is going to be *gachinko*."

Kinboshi (Gold star)
> A beautiful girl. A fairly pretty girl is a *Ginboshi*, or silver star.
>
> "Look at that *Kinboshi* sitting over there!"

Gots'an (Thanks for the delicious meal)
> Used for a wide range of things. It means being treated.
>
> "Boss, here's the check for this bar. *Gots'an desu!*"

Shika kimeru (Make like a deer)
> One card of a classic Japanese game shows a deer

looking off to one side. This terms means to ignore something or someone.

"The other night he didn't go out drinking with us because he said he had to work late. It turns out he really had a date!"

"Really? let's make like a deer for a while."

Shoppai (Salty)

Severe, uncompromising, stingy

"My grades are salty this semester."

Tako ni naru (Make like an octopus)

To be snooty.

"She's making like an octopus these days."

Tanimachi (Sponsor)

"Hey everyone! Our *Tanimachi* is footing the bill! Let's hear it: *Gots'an desu!*"

Chusha (Shot or injection)

The little something extra necessary for receiving a special favor.

"The shot for passing that professor's class is a bottle of whisky."

Haataro (foolish boy) *Haachan* (foolish girl)

"You 'haachan!' How many times do I have to tell you something?"

Bariki (Horsepower)

Liquor.

"Let's leave at five and go get some horsepower!"

TV and Radio Live Broadcasts

Sumo appreciation begins with TV broadcasts. You can see the bouts up close and get a running commentary. The vantage point is better than most seats at Kokugikan Hall and your sofa is more capacious. It's the best seat in the house.

NHK broadcasts live sumo from 3:05 pm to 6:00 pm during tournaments, beginning with the latter half of the *juryo* bouts. If you want more, tune in to NHK satellite broadcasts beginning at 1:00 pm, which start off with *sandanme*. It is interesting to watch these novices who still do not have the power or control of *makuuchi* wrestlers. This is followed by *makushita* and *juryo* divisions. You get a chance here to make your guesses as to who the future stars will be.

Another advantage of the satellite broadcasts is that they feature English-language commentary. The great allure is that it is NOT simultaneous interpretation of the regular NHK Japanese commentary. NHK managed to come up with a handful of native English speakers who are sumo experts (they are also contributors to the *Sumo World* magazine) and full of facts about the wrestlers themselves and the sport in general. One Japanese announcer is on hand to give "*Hanamichi* Reports," or what seem to be updates from the Japanese-language broadcasts, but these do not add much. BS Channel 2 broadcasts from 1 to 5 pm. Change to BS Channel 1 from 5 to 6.

For busy people, TV Asahi offers the Grand Sumo Digest at 11.15 pm. The best parts of the day's bouts are offered here. Another possibility for people who cannot plant themselves in front of the TV all afternoon is the NHK radio broadcast. Switch on the radio and enjoy the commentary and descriptions as you work.

Enjoy Tournaments Overseas

Sumo is also popular in other countries. Britain's Channel 4 carries TV broadcasts. NBC offers English-language radio sumo to the mainland U.S. and Hawaii.

NHK's international radio transmits Japanese-language broadcasts from 5 to 6 pm during tournaments. If you've got the right radio, you can listen to sumo anywhere in the world!

SUMO IN LONDON

Nicknames for the Wrestlers

Sumo is quite popular overseas. There are pockets of fans in places where there are large populations of ethnic Japanese, such as Hawaii and Brazil. In recent years, it has also come to be loved by the English as well. In October 1991, the London Grand Sumo Tournament was held over five days at the Royal Albert Hall as a part of a Japanese festival.

The reaction of the English to the essential allure of sumo was extremely interesting. Sumo, a phenomena of Eastern history and culture, seemed to appeal to the English and their love of tradition and ritual.

English fans were aware *rikishi* were fat and wore their hair in topknots, but they were dumbfounded to find out just how big they were. Bigger even than British rugby players. Local newspapers had a field day with Konishiki, the largest *rikishi* in sumo history.

It did not take long for Londoners to come up with nicknames for the *rikishi* based on their looks and habits. Konishiki was dubbed "Dump Truck." Hokutoumi became "Bull Dog." (In Japan, he is known as "Pochi," a common name for a dog.) Diminutive and nimble Mainoumi was known as "Mighty Mouse." Terao, with his menacing good looks, was "Typhoon." And Mitoizumi, the flinger of liberal amounts of salt, was known as "The Salt Shaker."

Favorites are the Same Everywhere

The English liked Terao and Kirishima, with their "soup" type muscular physiques and fearless expressions. The now-retired Chiyonofuji also found his popularity at all-new heights. At the closing ceremonies in London, fans yelled "Give us the Wolf!" (Chiyonofuji's nickname in Japan) The wax museum in London is even planning to add a figure of this great *rikishi* to its collection.

Fans also loved the smaller *rikishi*, such as Mainoumi and Kyokudozan. Apparently, the English have always had a weakness for underdogs. This is not to say that they did not like the big *rikishi*, such as Konishiki, Akebono, and The Salt Shaker Mitoizumi, who found themselves more popular abroad than at home. They were seen as the tough guys with soft hearts.

Come to think of it, the English mentality must work much the same as does the Japanese. The English crowds went wild over the stare-downs, the speed of the *rikishis'* movements and their overall might. They took a great interest in the bow-twirling ceremony and called out *"Yoisho!"* when the *yokozuna* made their entrances. Britons needed no encouragement to appreciate sumo.

The *rikishi* were caught up in the enthusiasm of the crowd, displaying unusually light footwork. Certainly no Japanese crowd has ever been favored with Hokutoumi's strongman pose. (Although a similar display of human emotion would be a welcome addition to a regular tournament!) The London press was also fairly accu-

117

rate in its reportage of the cultural side of sumo. They intelligently discussed the "chanko stew," the "dohyo ring!" and the "warm-up stance." It should never be said that only Japanese, who have been born and raised on sumo, can appreciate it fully.

The Betting Behind the Boom

Another factor behind the popularity of sumo in England was the legal gambling system. Sumo bouts, along with other overseas sports, have long been handled by bookmakers. For years, the bet-happy Britons have rejoiced and mourned at the outcome of Japanese sumo. Thanks to the bookmakers, there was little chance that sumo would not be a hit when it arrived on the London scene. There were plenty of fans who consulted the odds before choosing their favorites.

The Ring with 100 Supporting Columns

The Royal Albert Hall is a classic hall built in 1871 by Queen Victoria for her husband Prince Albert. It has wonderful acoustics. The voices of the announcers and the sound of the wooden clappers rang out to the audience. The final bout had the feel of an operatic climax. During the bouts, the lights were all lowered except for those over the ring, giving the BBC broadcasts a totally different flavor from those from the Kokugikan Hall. This new atmosphere suited the sport admirably.

A sumo ring had never been made in the Royal Albert Hall before, and it was a monumental task. 100 supporting columns were built under the ring to support the weight of forty tons of dirt and five tons of *rikishi* assembled for the ring-entering ceremony. Local staff studied videotapes of ring preparation ahead of time. Soil was searched for everywhere, with the final choice being dirt from an area near Heathrow International Airport. The final product was finally achieved by adding 30% sand.

An English-language Tournament Magazine

There is an English-language magazine designed for non-Japanese sumo fans. The title is *Sumo World*. The feature story is always a detailed discussion of the most recent tournament including a wealth of photographs. Find out the vital statistics of your favorite *rikishi*, learn about sumo customs and history.

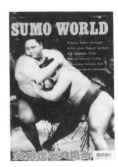

One of its most innovative items is a *banzuke* ranking chart for the next tournament in both *kanji* and English. This magazine is a must for English-speaking sumo fans! Issues come out bimonthly, just before regularly scheduled tournaments. The magazine is available at the Foreign Press Club, Ryogoku Kokugikan, the American Pharmacy, Kino-kuniya, Maruzen, and other book and magazine shops where English publications are sold. The magazine is ¥650 an issue or ¥4,500 for a one-year subscription. You can get it at the "Foreign books" corner of bookstores and major hotels.

LET'S VISIT THE KOKUGIKAN HALL

The Tournament Schedule

What happens when watching sumo on TV is not enough? The only option left is to go to the Kokugikan Hall to see a tournament. There are six official tournaments a year.

Annual Schedule of Official Tournaments

Hatsu-basho—The First Tournament
 Begins the second Sunday in January
 Ryogoku Kokugikan Hall, Tokyo

Haru-basho—The Spring Tournament
 Begins the second Sunday in March
 Osaka City Gymnasium, Osaka

Natsu-basho—The Summer Tournament
 Begins the second Sunday in May
 Ryogoku Kokugikan Hall, Tokyo

Nagoya-basho—The Nagoya Tournament
 Begins the first Sunday in July
 Aichi Prefectural Gymnasium, Nagoya

Aki-basho—The Autumn Tournament
 Begins the second Sunday in September
 Ryogoku Kokugikan Hall, Tokyo

Kyushu-basho—The Kyushu Tournament
 Begins the second Sunday in November
 Fukuoka International Center, Fukuoka

Tournaments always begin on the second Sunday of the month in which they are scheduled, except for the Nagoya Tournament which begins on the first Sunday.

Tickets for regularly-scheduled tournaments go on sale about a month ahead of time. (The exact dates vary, but the first sales date is usually a Saturday.) Tickets are sold at Play Guide, Ticket Saison, Ticket Pia, JTB and Nihon Ryoko travel agencies, and at the Kokugikan Hall.

Posters hung in train stations advertise ticket sales, as do ads in sumo periodicals. These magazines are also the best source of information on exhibition sumo tournaments.

Types of Seats and Their Prices

Seats have different grades, just like in professional baseball. And it is just as difficult to get hold of tickets for the best seats. Learning the different seats (and their prices) is a good way to learn about the Kokugikan Hall itself.

Tamari-seki

An extra-special seat with a price tag of ¥12,500. It is roughly equivalent to a seat behind home plate at a baseball game. The seats themselves are cushions positioned behind the judges. Another name for these seats is "sand spray." This is a dangerous place to sit because you may find a *rikishi*, along with some sand, in your lap. In fact, there have been fans who were injured when *rikishi* fell on top of them. Rumor has it that the Japan Sumo Association has *tamari-seki* insurance policies. At any rate, it is an exciting place to be during a tournament.

Unfortunately, these seats are difficult to come by. The Kokugikan tea shops sell them to paying members (¥500,000 annual dues) who have bought blocks of *masu-seki* sets (see below) over a period of years. These are the only seats in which eating and drinking are prohibited (try to imagine a *yakitori* skewer encountering the bare flesh of a losing wrestler).

Masu-seki (Box seats)

These are seats sectioned off into blocks of two to four seats. Think of them as comparable to infield box seats at a baseball stadium. *Masu-seki* have three price levels depending upon their vicinity to the ring. A seats are ¥9500, B seats ¥8500, and C seats ¥7500.

The best of these seats are controlled by the tea shops (Sumo Service Guide Center), and sold to large corporations, who use them to entertain important guests, and travel agencies and hotels, which sell them as part of their own tour "packages." These customers purchase seats for entire tournaments. The public rarely gets a chance at *masu-seki*, and fans can stand in line all night with no guarantee of getting these prize tickets. (The Kokugikan Hall is located in Sumida Ward in Tokyo and it always reserves a few *masu-seki* seats for local residents.) *Masu-seki* seats are sold in blocks of two to four (with the smaller blocks usually the ones leftover for the public), so, theoretically, the most you would pay would be about ¥38,000. Buying them from a tea shop, however, also involves the purchase of a set of tea cups, a box lunch, snacks, *sake*, poster, and so on. In no time at all, the price is pushed up to as much as ¥100, 000.

There are surely many fans who would do anything, no matter what the price, to sit in one of these seats, but few individuals ever get a chance. Better to think of them as cushions with a corporate contract.

The tea shops could not stay in business without being able to offer this combination of tickets and refreshments. Allowing the tea shops control of *masu-seki* seats is a policy of the sumo industry for keeping ticket sales stable even if sumo popularity should decline. As reasonable as this may seem, it still angers normal fans. Even sumo-stable friends and family have a hard time getting *masu-seki* seats.

Each ticket bought from a tea shop has a number identifying which shop made the sale. The ticket holder goes to that tea shop where a *kimono*-clad woman or man wearing *hakama* will lead the way to the seat itself bearing the souvenirs included in the ticket price. It is a normal practice to give these attendants a tip of about ¥2000. Forget that tip, and the attendant will give you a glare which seems to say "Come back in ten years when you've grown up!" If you are ever invited to a tournament and provided with *masu-seki* seats, don't begrudge the tip, it is one of the more subtle aspects of sumo appreciation.

Chairs —A seats

¥7000. A seats are the first rows of the balcony. Roughly comparable to infield seats. The chairs have arm rests and a tray for drinks. You also get a bottle opener. These seats are more comfortable than *masu-seki*. The view is not quite as good, but it is easier to get in and out. Many of these seats, however, are sold in blocks and include refreshments, making them expensive as well as rare.

Chairs—B seats

¥5000. B seats are the middle rows of the balcony. There is no tray and the view is not nearly as good as on TV.

Chairs—C seats

¥2300. You are now sitting in the "outfield" of the hall. Your "chair" might more accurately be described as a bench. Still, you have made it to the Kokugikan Hall and not spent your entire fortune to do so.

Non-reserved Seats

¥1500. The back benches. There are 400 of these seats which can only be purchased on the day they are to be used. Your regular, run-of-the-mill sumo fan will stand in line early in the morning to get these tickets. With luck a few B or C tickets may be left.

Buying Tickets

The more popular sumo gets, the harder it is to buy tickets. The day before tickets go on sale for a regularly-scheduled tournament, an average of 700 people wait in line all night. (3,000 fans waited in line overnight to purchase tickets for the 1991 Autumn Tournament.) Any available *masu-seki* seats sell out during the morning hours, all A seats are gone by 2 pm, and all B seats by 4 pm.

It goes without saying that the better the seat, the quicker the tickets disappear. This is especially true for the first, middle, and last days of any tournament, all of which are Sundays. Weekday tickets go quickly for the latter half of a tournament. Recently fans will take any day or seat they can buy and consider themselves lucky to have done so.

Ticket Information

Kokugikan Telephone Reservation: 03-3622-1100

Sumo Annai-sho: 03-3625-2111

Ticket Saison: 03-5990-9999

Ticket Pia: 03-5237-9999

CN Play Guide: 03-3257-9999

KOKUGIKAN
WATCHING

Watch Out for Rush Hour Trains

Sumo fans love to buy non-reserved seats at the Kokugikan Hall. Despite the fact that the giant *rikishi* will look no bigger than grains of rice, the price is right and the opportunity is there.

Non-reserved seats are only sold on the day they can be used. They are popular with people who have not managed to buy advance-sale reserved seats and sumo freaks who attend several days of each tournament. These are the tickets I recommend to novice sumo fans for their first visit to the Kokugikan Hall.

The ticket window opens at 9 a.m. Sumo is so popular lately that purchasers should plan on being in line at least an hour ahead of time, even on weekdays, to guarantee getting a seat.

The Kokugikan Hall is located in front of the Ryogoku Station on the Sobu Line. When I made my first trip, I went equipped with the information that I should arrive about 8 a.m., but there was something I had forgotten to consider—the morning rush hour traffic headed for Tokyo. Like a country boy new to the big city, I had hung my camera around my neck, and the press of humanity in the crowded train dug the strap into my skin. I had intended to leave the train when it arrived at Ryogoku Station, moving with the flow of the other disembarking passengers—another mistake. Very few commuters work in the area and nobody got off the train. By the time I managed to call out and plead to be let through, it was too late. I was already on my way to the next station. Becoming a sumo spectator is no simple task.

Advice

Keep your belongings to a minimum and wear comfortable clothes. Some people may feel a need to dress up for the occasion, but only do this if you have a reserved seat.

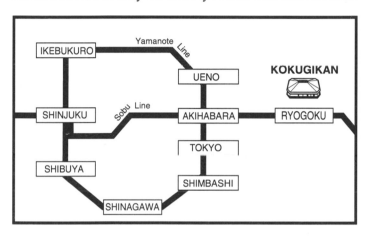

You Can Smell Sumo from the Station

In front of the station a concession booth sells pre-paid telephone and train cards complete with pictures of sumo wrestlers. These are sold by Japan Railway employees. Everybody in the neighborhood makes a profit from sumo, even the railroads!

I went around to a convenience store behind the station. There was, of course, a poster advertising the current tournament posted near the cash register. I even thought I could hear the sound of the sumo drums in the distance. Ryogoku is a sumo-oriented neighborhood.

The Kokugikan Hall is right in front of the west entrance to the station. There is a path that goes directly from the Hall to the station for the benefit of spectators. There is also a big sign that says "Buy Your Return Ticket Ahead of Time." About 10,000 people can fit into the Kokugikan Hall, and one can imagine the chaos at the station after the day's bouts are over.

The South Gate is in the Safety Zone

The Kokugikan Hall is a busy place during regularly-scheduled tournaments. Colorful banners bearing the names of wrestlers are raised and you can hear the constant beating of the huge, outdoor drum. That was what I had heard from the convenience store. Even the public telephones on the sidewalk are shaped like miniature Kokugikan Halls.

The line quickly backing up along the sidewalk was that of fans waiting to buy non-reserved tickets for the day's bouts. There was a group of three middle-aged women chatting away, an old man by himself, some young foreigners, and student couples. It is clear even here that sumo has a broad appeal.

By the time I found it, the end of the line was at the South Gate of the hall. This is the wrestlers' entrance. It seemed awfully far from the ticket booth. Standing in front of me were three middle-aged men. One of them started counting the number of people in line.

Man A: There're about 120 ahead of us.

Man B: It's getting harder to get tickets; just like the Seibu Lions baseball games.

Man C: We'll be lucky to get two tickets each today.

It finally dawned on me. These were not men who just happened to love both sumo and baseball. They were scalpers. They were planning to buy their tickets and then get back in line to buy another one. At any rate, they had inadvertently let me know that I would be able to get the one ticket I needed to get inside.

Advice

You will know you are absolutely safe if you are near the South Gate before the ticket window opens.

Scalpers and Security Guards

Within a few minutes, other scalpers arrived on the scene and began working their way into the line. After the first scalpers bought their tickets, they were casually let back into line by their friends farther to the rear.

Quick as a wink, the security guards were on the scene:

"Everybody waits their turn. You just bought a ticket, didn't you? The rules say only one to a customer. Out you go."

The security guards were polite but firm even though they knew who the scalpers were. The scalpers themselves, grinned 'innocently' and tried to laugh off their 'mistake.'

"I just wanted to buy a ticket for a friend. But I see now that it's not allowed."

The well-practiced performance was an amusing start to the day's proceedings. But remember, not even non-scalpers can buy more than one ticket a person.

Cheering Do's and Don'ts

While I was waiting in line for my ticket, small groups of *rikishi* began to appear. I could hear the clip-clop of their geta before I saw them, dressed in *yukata* and carrying their possessions in *furoshiki*. They were the *jonokuchi* wrestlers who were first on the day's program.

"Good luck!" A middle-aged woman who probably didn't even know their names called out words of encouragement. It was a heart-warming sight.

The only rule to remember here is not to call out "Good luck, *Sekitori*!" No *sekitori* (in other words, wrestlers of *juryo* rank and above) make their appearance this early in the morning.

Advice

In Japanese society, nobody takes offense if they are addressed as "Chief," or "Boss." The world of sumo, however, is in a realm of its own, and mistakes concerning rank are offences that are not taken lightly. The feelings of *rikishi* are easily wounded and understandably too, considering the sacrifices involved in achieving this often short-lived status. If you want to see your favorite *rikishi* as he enters the hall, the rule is to wait quietly by the South Gate.

If You Get Sick

A sign by the South Gate states that the Sumo Association Clinic will attend to the public. Very few people realize that there is a doctor's office at the Kokugikan Hall. So, if you begin to feel faint while you are waiting in line, don't worry, there is someone to take care of you.

Advice

Clinic or no clinic, don't risk keeling over before you buy your ticket; your trip will have been in vain. Make sure you eat a good breakfast before you start out!

Special Trophies

I finally got my ¥1500 ticket. I could enter the hall right away, or come back later at my leisure. I decided to go straight in and see what was there.

Right inside the entrance was an impressive Isuzu four-wheel-drive car. This was a special prize for the tournament winner. In the show case near the entrance, the winner's trophy was displayed. The one you may have seen on TV on the last day of a tournament. There was also a glass trophy filled with pickled plums. This was the Fukui Prefecture Governor's Prize. The trophy filled with dried *shiitake* mushrooms was the Oita Shiitake Producers' Prize. The bronze cow, a symbol of Miyazaki beef, was the Miyazaki Prefecture Governor's Prize. The tournament winner receives not only the prize money and huge trophy, but all sorts of other prizes. (I wonder what they do with all the plums and *shiitake*?)

The Oita Shiitake Producer's Prize.
A glass trophy filled with dried shiitake mushrooms.

To the side of one aisle was the Morinaga Ballot Box. On an empty Morinaga candy box, spectators write their name, address and the bout they are most interested in seeing, and put it in the ballot box. Morinaga tallies up

Prizes for the Winning *Rikishi*

The Emperor's Cup.
The Winner's Flag.
The Prime Minister's Cup and prize money.
The Winner's Portrait (a portrait displayed in the Kokugikan Hall).
Prize money from the Mainichi Shimbun Newspaper.
Friendship cups from various countries.
NHK Cup and prize money.

There are also awards from corporations, foundations, and local governments, including a wide variety of unique prizes: rice, meat, vegetables, cars, and so on. The United Arab Emirates Friendship Cup includes a year's supply of gasoline. The puppies of Tosa fighting dogs have also been given as prizes. These are dogs bred in the Tosa area of Shikoku which have traditionally engaged in fights with *rikishi*.

TV broadcasts are usually terminated before these unusual trophies can be presented to the winner. So, if you ever get a chance to go to the Kokugikan Hall on the final day of a tournament, be sure to stay until the very end of the day's activities.

the votes and gives a prize to the *rikishi* in the most popular bout. They then draw the names of three spectators to receive an additional prize.

There are more prizes for the fans. I saw lottery boxes —four on the first floor and one near the second-floor exit. Winners may receive a travel coupon (the *Yokozuna* Prize), a framed picture of the winning wrestler (*Ozeki* Prize), or a towel with a wrestler's handprint (*Sekiwake* Prize).

Advice

Don't miss out on these special services for fans; you never know what you might end up taking home at the end of the day.

Be an Educated Fan

To the side of the entrance hallway is the Sumo Museum. This museum has tens of thousands of items, including portraits and photographs of *rikishi*, possessions of wrestlers who have died, and so on. The museum rotates exhibits every month.

The Japan Sumo Association is not amused when private aspects of *rikishi* are aired for the public in an entertaining fashion, but in the museum, the Association has seen fit to demonstrate the fact that twenty cups of rice could fit inside the *tabi* footwear of Edo era wrestler Raiden. You may also enjoy seeing the report card of former *yokozuna* Futabayama. (By the way, he got perfect marks in the first and second grades of elementary school.)

You will also find handprints, formal *kimono*, and other items that will wet your thirst for a day of sumo. Be sure not to miss the museum. If I were allowed one complaint, it would be to say that I would have liked to have seen everything the museum has in its possession.

Advice

Sumo is even more interesting when you are able to take a closer look at the wrestlers memorabilia. The Sumo Museum provides an excellent chance to do this.

The Museum is open everyday except Saturdays, holidays, and the New Year's holidays [Jan. 1-3]. It is free on non-tournament days. During tournaments, however, you must have a ticket to get in.

Sumo Souvenirs

The bouts had still not begun at 9 a.m. I peeked into the hall and found the ring full of people conferring and making preparations. I decided I would check out the souvenir stands.

Souvenir salespersons include friendly, grandmotherly types and young women who look as though they would be glad to be anywhere else. (I thought I had seen some of them before. Then I realized that they wore expressions identical to those of the women who work in the thousands of station Kiosks throughout the country.)

They also sell a variety of products that rival the station concessions. The multitude of offerings can be broken down into two categories: ① food and drink and ② souvenirs. While there is a wide array of souvenirs, you may not find many items with esthetic appeal, but looking them over is a good way to pass the time and a laugh is assured.

Advice

Do not look at souvenirs as a serious way of sharing your Kokugikan experience. Rather think of your purchases as a way to amuse your friends and family.

The Ranking Chart of Souvenirs

Yokozuna: Yakitori (Barbecued chicken on wooden skewers)

Kokugikan *yakitori* is popular because it is tasty even when eaten cold. In fact, they are probably prepared with the understanding that they will always be eaten cold. At ¥520 for five *yakitori,* the *tsukune,* or ground meat, variety is especially good. Eat a few while sipping *sake* to enjoy the bouts even more!

Ozeki : Handprints

Signed handprints are a bargain at ¥260. Or so I thought, until I realized they had been mass produced. A casual glance, however, will not give the secret away. A fun gift anybody would enjoy.

Sekiwake: Sumo Apron

A simple apron printed with "National sports in Japan sumo RYOGOKU KOKUGIKAN (sic)." ¥1550. No prizes for guessing where you bought this little number. A perfect gift for your mother.

Komusubi: Ryogoku Paper Sumo Game

You'll chuckle over the catch phrases printed on these. "Enjoyment for the whole family!" "New Feeling in the Ring!" "The fights are more fun than ever!" The paper sumo games are made by an affiliate of Lion, the home-product maker. Lion and paper sumo? Is there any connection here? Actually, Lion headquarters are located across the street from the hall. ¥720.

Maegashira 1st class: O-sumo-san T-shirts

Colorfully illustrated T-shirts in children's sizes. From ¥1550.

Maegashira 2nd class: *Uchiwa* Fans

Complete with an illustration of a sumo wrestler. A nice present, but ¥720 is steep for a garden-variety fan.

Maegashira 3rd class: Lollipop

¥300. No matter how much you lick it, the face of the friendly sumo wrestler never disappears. Kids will love it.

Maegashira 4th class: Grand Sumo Playing Cards

¥1550. Photographs of *rikishi* are printed on the cards. The wrestlers with the higher ranks are kings and

queens. Once again the ranking chart prevails. (Is it fair to have the head *gyoji* Kimura Shonosuke as the joker?)

Maegashira 5th class: The Masculine Mug

Printed with a *rikishi's* name and caricature. Good value at ¥1250. (The likeness of Takanohana was not very good.)

Maegashira 6th class: Seishu Hakushika Kokugikan

Canned *sake*. Goes well with *yakitori*. A big favorite among the men. ¥350.

Juryo: Gekkeikan Cap Ace Kokugikan

Sake in a plastic bottle. It comes with a cup and is deco-

rated with wrestlers. It is quite an impressive item, but the smell of the plastic bothered me. ¥350.

Makushita: Sumo *Bento* (Boxed lunch)

This is a generic Japanese boxed lunch. Use of third-class ingredients prevents a higher ranking. ¥850.

Sandanme: Gunbai Senbei

If you look carefully, you will see that these rice crackers are shaped like the fan held by the *gyoji*. ¥520.

Jonidan: Binoculars

Two prices: ¥850 and ¥1500. This is a product created with the fans in the back rows in mind. I will admit that they come close to serving their function, but best to think of them as disposable toys (especially the cheaper ones.)

The *Tamari-seki* Seats are Empty

While I stood marvelling at the souvenirs, the *jonokuchi* bouts got underway, and I headed for my seat. I was surprised at how empty the hall was during the morning hours. Staying in my assigned seat in the very back rows of an empty hall seemed unnaturally well-behaved, so I headed for the front-row cushions.

The ground floor was fairly empty except for the judges and the *rikishi* waiting their turns. Nothing like the crowd I was used to seeing on TV. The few spectators, however, all looked to be serious fans. I glanced around and noticed a foreigner studying the day's program and an older man enjoying his first cup of *sake* in the *masu-seki* seats. The few paying very close attention to the action were most likely the parents or close relatives of *jonokuchi rikishi*.

The hall is open, but bouts have not yet begun. Preparation began right after this photograph was taken.

Advice

Sitting in seats other than those for which you have tickets is prohibited, but there is no one to come around and check. There should be no objection to brief occupation of an empty seat if you mind your manners. Do not leave any trash. Return, eventually, to your own seat. Put the cushion back in place when you leave. Certainly any fan enthusiastic enough to turn out for these earliest bouts is capable of following a few rules.

A sprinkling of spectators are on hand for the *jonokuchi* bouts.

The main bouts complete with the traditional banner recognizing a sold-out house.

first floor

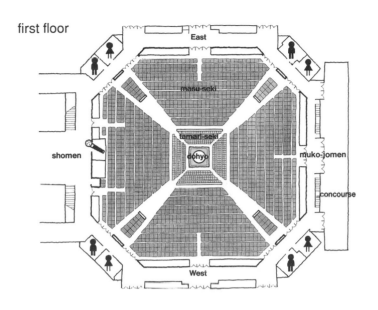

second floor

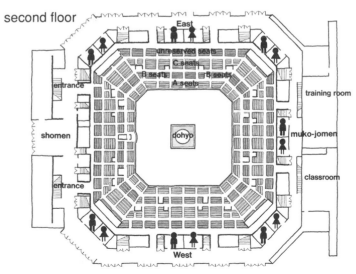

147

You Will Never See
Jonokuchi on TV

One look at the *rikishi-in-waiting* told me this was green-horn sumo. Most of these boys were fresh out of junior high school and still had close-cropped heads. No matter how big they were, they were still not strong. Overweight was the main impression. Some looked so weak that I thought even I could have beaten them. The announcers and *gyoji* were also beginners. Their voices did not carry and they did not yet have the rhythm down. When they called out "*Nishi* . . ." ("On the west side . . ."), the final vowel stopped short and their voices cracked. I've heard drunks in *karaoke* bars do better.

Another good look at the wrestlers waiting at the head of the line, however, showed a seriousness belying the length of their careers. I could see the ones towards the end of the line fooling around, and then watched the change in their expressions as they got closer to the ring.

A few had their own cheering sections comprised of family and close friends. They definitely made up in enthusiasm what they lacked in numbers.

The bouts themselves were uninspiring. The boys had been taught a few basics, but they did not have much in the way of technique. It would have been interesting to see some leg moves, but most of the action was just pushing back and forth in the center of the ring.

Jonokuchi provided a sort of culture shock after having watched nothing but *makuuchi* bouts on TV. On the few occasions when skill was exhibited, the fans responded with warm applause.

Jonidan

The *jonidan* wrestlers demonstrated a speed and technique that more resembled sumo. The wrestlers were also bigger and their hair was longer. Definitely a mixed bag of ability, with many lopsided combinations.

Sometimes a wrestler with obvious talent stood out. The man next to me said that he got his greatest enjoyment from making notes on these *rikishi* and then watching them move up through the ranks.

Serious Sumo begins at *Sandanme*

Sandanme wrestlers provided a performance on par with the high school baseball tournaments at Koshien Sta-

The *Torikumi-hyo*

Upon entering the Kokugikan Hall, everyone receives a program of the day's events. It also includes the names of referees and judges, and the *rikishi* who will perform the bow-twirling ceremony. Use this chart to match the names of wrestlers with their faces. Also printed on the chart are the names of sponsors of special prizes, win-loss records, and the seventy official moves.

dium. NHK satellite broadcasts begin with *sandanme* bouts. Wrestlers still did not have the technique of *makuuchi* wrestlers, but their faces had begun to look tougher and more experienced, and they all sported modest topknots. Every once in a while, the crowd was favored with a deft performance.

Bring Your Binoculars and Transistor Radio

During the *juryo* bouts, the hall began to fill up. It was time to return to my seat in the non-reserved outback. My view was now greatly obscured.

In the *tamari-seki* seats, I was able to see the hair on the wrestlers' legs and any bruises on their backsides. From the rear of the balcony, the only thing that was apparent was that somebody down below was engaged in sumo.

To improve your lot, it is a good idea to bring binoculars. Bird-watching binoculars with 8x magnification are just about right given the distance and the object of observation. Hand movement is not particularly distracting. The lights go up for the later bouts making spectating much easier.

I took my own binoculars out. Now the view was good enough to see the wrestlers' cheeks vibrating at the moment of impact. I could even see the indentations on their legs.

A radio will make the bouts even more interesting.

You can hear the NHK broadcasts made from inside the hall itself. The radio announcer will get the results to you more quickly than the hall PA system, and, of course, you will get a full explanation. Your eyes will tire if you use binoculars too long. Wait till the referee has declared

---

Another Use for Binoculars

I enjoyed using my binoculars to watch the fans watching the bouts. There were people in the coveted *masu-seki* seats gobbling down their lunches with their backs to the action. There were some fans who looked like small businessmen who had been provided with tickets by their main supplier. A young couple was so engrossed in each other that I thought they had wandered in by mistake. Another party looked to be pompous executives showing off their top seats to their girlfriends from their favorite bars. Anyway, you can get an idea (or imagine you are getting an idea) of who gets the best seats.

In the back rows, I saw a modern phenomenon visible at every Japanese sporting event from baseball to horse racing; the over-reacting, jumping-up-and-down girls (often in pairs). There were also groups of high-school students on their school trip who found it hard to sit still, and, of course, women of a mature age with amazingly loud voices. All characteristic Japanese (although there were also a few noisy foreigners).

At any rate, watching the fans is almost as much fun as watching the bouts.

---

matta-nashi and use the binoculars until the action is over. It also helps to roll up a magazine and place it on your lap to use as an arm rest to keep the binoculars steady.

From the *tamari-seki* seats you can count the hairs on the wrestlers' legs.

Masu-seki seats. No danger of a wrestler landing on you.

Advice

Keep up with the action using your binoculars and radio. The improved quality of your experience will be amazing. People around radio holders constantly ask for updates.

The view is still good from the balcony "A" seats.

A sad story: the view from the non-reserved seats.

The Art of Entering the Ring

After the *juryo* bouts end, there is a short break before the main attraction begins. The *makuuchi* bouts are called *nakairi* (or "entering the center"... or "getting down to business"). And when listening to the live broadcast the announcer will say "And now for the nakairi bouts."

Nakairi begins at 4 p.m. By that time the hall is just about full and the live NHK broadcast begins. First, the *makuuchi* wrestlers, up through the *ozeki* rank, enter. During this ring-entering ceremony, the wrestlers wear an apron called a *kesho-mawashi* (or decorative loincloth). These aprons are very colorful and sport a variety of designs. There was one depicting the Sapporo Clock

Tower; its owner was obviously from Hokkaido. A wrestler from Toyama Prefecture had a design of a snow grouse on his. Some apron designs are abstract, some bear classical calligraphy motifs.

Next, it was time for the *yokozuna* to enter, each accompanied by his herald and sword bearer. This is a unique ceremony. The *yokozuna* have huge ropes tied around their aprons, and they go through the *chirichozu* motions and stamp. The crowd cheered enthusiastically as they finally got a glimpse of these sumo stars. There were calls of *"Yoisho!"* and the excitement was at its height.

The rope worn by a *yokozuna* is made by all the *rikishi* in his stable before a Tokyo tournament. The center of

the rope is linen and copper wire. Its length is 4 m and weighs about 20 kg. The circumference is 45 cm at its thickest. (Long ago, the width was less.)

The rope is tied behind the wrestler into either a loop, called *unryu* (dragon in the clouds—the most popular style among recent *yokozuna*), or into a large bow, called *shiranui* (mysterious lights on the sea). These names apply not only to the rope but also to the motions the *yokozuna* goes through as a part of the ceremony. In other words, if he chooses the *unryu* style of ring-entering (as has *yokozuna* Akebono), his rope will be tied in *unryu* fashion and his motions will be *unryu* motions.

Kesho-mawashi 1

The *kesho-mawashi* aprons are given to wrestlers. Some wrestlers have said that they will never forget the feeling they had when they received their first apron as a new *juryo*-rank wrestler.

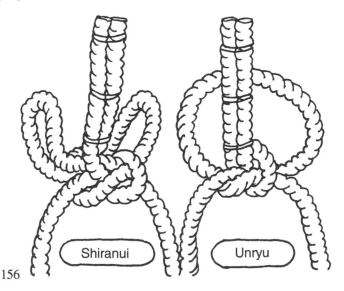

Shiranui   Unryu

The cost of these aprons start at a mind-boggling ¥1 million and have been known to climb to a dizzying height of ¥150 million for an apron decorated with diamonds.

Aprons are received from a variety of sources: individual sponsors, support groups for individual *rikishi*, and stable support groups. Almost all ex-college sumo *rikishi* receive aprons from their alma maters. Popular wrestlers have a large selection to choose from. Avid fans will be able to tell at a glance whether or not a *rikishi* is sporting a brand-new apron.

Kesho-mawashi 2

The designs on the aprons are as beautiful as tapestries and even more interesting. Careful observation will often reveal the hometown of its owner, his image, the good (or bad) taste of his sponsor, and the sponsor's financial position. The name of the beneficiary is woven into the hem of the apron. Be sure to check out the design, the quality, the name, and make your own analysis!

The most frequent depictions are of a wrestler's birthplace. The American *rikishi* Konishiki has an apron with an illustration of the Statue of Liberty. Akebono, hailing from Hawaii, has one with a hibiscus woven into the design. Akinoshima's apron depicts the Japanese maples of his native Hiroshima. Daijuyama has the *nishikigoi* carp of Niigata on his. If the colors on some of the aprons were any more vivid, they might be mistaken for picture postcards.

Mitoizumi has an apron with a depiction of Mito City's Kairaku-en Park and plum blossoms. I had to smile at the Tokyoite Wakanohana's apron—Tokyo

Tower, a high-rise building, and a linear motor car—identical to the pictures of "Tokyo of the Future" we used to see thirty years ago!

There are also aprons that act as advertisements. Aprons of Kushimaumi and Daikiko carry the emblems of their universities. Takatoriki has an apron with a huge Pepsicola logo. An automobile manufacturer sent Tomoefuji an apron with an illustration of Mt. Fuji as a background for a crane truck.

Enhance the pleasure of the ring-entering ceremony by keeping your eyes on the aprons.

Cheering the Bouts

When the *makuuchi* bouts began the cheering became more exuberant. Some veterans, however, complain that an increase in "fairweather" fans has led to a decrease in refined spectating. Groups of young girls are in greater evidence. They stand up and screech at the top of their lungs, making it impossible to follow the action.

It is not good manners to intrude on the pleasure of other spectators. It is one thing to encourage your favorite wrestlers, but it is another to heckle their opponents. I was chagrined to see one man throwing his cushion into the ring during the final bout of the day.

Good cheering helps build excitement, not dampen it. Sometimes, though, hecklers have their day. Once, just before a tournament, a certain wrestler was caught in the middle of a scandalous affair. When he entered the ring for his bout, one of the fans in the *masu-seki* seats called out, "Go for it, lover boy!" and the crowd broke out in laughter.

Choosing Favorites

There are numerous reasons for choosing a favorite *rikishi,* but it is bound to fit into one of the five categories below.

SAME HOMETOWN

A strong *rikishi* is the pride of his hometown. This is a tradition that has carried on since the days of sumo *sechie,* and is a proof of the Japanese "island-nation psyche." Announcers always give the name of a *rikishi* and his home prefecture. (Do you non-Japanese fans feel any different when you come across a *rikishi* from your own country?)

Japanese who move out of their native prefectures, whether to Tokyo or a foreign country, may start up or join already-existing *kenjin-kai* (or "group for people from the same prefecture"). If people from the same prefecture meet on a trip abroad, it is grounds for instant friendship. This affection for the old hometown and each and everyone of its residents holds true for sumo fans as well.

THE UNDERDOG

Ever since the age of the diminutive hero, Minamoto no Yoshitsune, Japanese have rooted for the hard-working soul in a disadvantaged position. When the smaller *rikishi*, such as Kyokudozan or Mainoumi, enter the ring, the applause increases. On other hand however, the *ex-yokozuna* Kitanoumi, didn't inspire such a vigorous response as fans found it difficult to warm to this mighty giant with the sullen expression.

GOOD LOOKS

Young women will often go for the handsome guy. Popularity does not last long, however, unless the pretty face is backed up with a certain amount of power. Through the ages, women cheering on handsome *rikishi* have helped build enthusiasm for the sport, but they often go from one favorite to the next. Nowadays, there seems to be a trend towards baseball.

There is also a soft spot in fans' hearts for *rikishi* on the opposite end of the scale, the "mascot" types, adorable for their pudgy mugs. Akebono, Konishiki, and the ex-Asashio, all have large followings.

HERO WORSHIP

Everyone loves the dedicated, humble, and extremely strong wrestler. Heroes who have attracted the generic sumo fan include Raiden, the legendary *rikishi* of the Edo era, Futabayama, who won 69 straight bouts, and Chiyonofuji, who received the Japanese Award of Honor. However, probably the most famous of them all was Taiho; he was held in such high esteem by the public that he was part of a popular saying: "There are three things all Japanese like—tamagoyaki eggs, the Giants baseball team, and Taiho."

THE CONNECTION

This type resembles the "same hometown" category, but transcends prefectural boundaries. You may happen to know a younger brother of a *rikishi*. Or a *rikishi* may be the friend of a friend's older brother. Any connection is a basis for a new favorite. Suppose a *rikishi's* sister moves into the vicinity. Before you know it, the entire neighborhood is cheering the new-found "friend." People will lean towards a *rikishi* whom they might have seen in a train station somewhere, or whose autograph they might have had a glimpse of.

Kensho Incentive Prizes

Another enjoyable aspect of *nakairi* bouts is the special prize called *kensho*. Sponsors pay a set amount of money on the bout of their choice, and the proceeds go to the winner. Certainly an enticing incentive for any *rikishi*.

The list of *kensho* is included in the program. And the sponsors also get their names on the colorful banners paraded around the ring by announcers before the bout they are intended for. It is, of course, a form of advertisement, and the sponsors are anticipating big results. Accordingly, they put their money down on a popular bout that fans are sure to have their eyes on. Some bouts will have more than ten *kensho*.

The PA system broadcasted the names of the sponsors and their slogans. Along with familiar corporate names-—Post Office Savings, Japan Travel Bureau, Ticket Pia, etc.—there were names of local *sushi* bars, neighborhood women's associations, and other groups with some connection to one of the *rikishi* in the bout. Listening carefully, I also picked out the names of makers of jock straps and band-aids, and others who make their living from sumo.

I enjoyed the slogan of Nichiro Inc., a company that often sponsors a *kensho* for Akebono's bouts: "Nichiro, the producer of Akebono Canned Salmon."

Apparently, any interested party can offer a *kensho*, but not under the name of an individual. The current price is ¥60,000. From this amount, the Japan Sumo Association takes 50% off the top to cover costs and income tax. Before this system was introduced, wrestlers would often spend all of their winnings before they discovered it was taxable income.

Kensho are one concrete measurement of a *rikishi's* popularity. There are, however, loyal sponsors who have stood by their favorites through thick and thin, putting *kensho* on their bouts for any number of years. In other words, *kensho* are not just advertisements for companies, but also aimed at public spiritedness.

Announcers are Walking Advertisements

Unfortunately, NHK, the government broadcasting company, never gives its viewers an opportunity to observe the unique *kensho* "commercials," but those who

MORE ON *KENSHO*

The history of *kensho* incentive prizes goes back to the beginning of sumo. Winning *rikishi* were given clothing, weapons, horses, land, and so on. In the Edo era, *kensho* were referred to as *nagebana* ("tossed flowers"). Fans threw money into the ring after a bout was over. The practice was abolished, however, when disgruntled spectators began throwing in their eating utensils, *hibachi* stoves, and other dangerous objects. After World War II, when food was scarce, wrestlers received meat and eggs as prizes.

After a bout with no *kensho* attached, the winning *rikishi* bows after hearing the *gyoji's* decision and leaves the ring. When he accepts a *kensho* prize, however, a *rikishi* makes three vertical chopping motions with his hand—first in the center, then to the right and the left. These motions represent cuts with a sword. It is a custom begun by a *rikishi* before World War II. It looked so graceful and dignified that others began to copy it, and it is now an accepted custom.

can read Japanese may notice that announcers have names of various companies printed on their outfits. Even NHK finds it difficult to totally avoid these ads as the announcers circle the ring, attending to their duties.

The reason that *kensho*-giving is allowed is that the Japan Sumo Association has had a longer relationship with these sponsoring corporations than with NHK. In other words, even the almighty NHK has failed to overpower the forces of Japanese duty and obligation (*giri-ninjo*).

At present, twelve different corporations are paying a total of several million yen a year for advertisement clothing. *Makuuchi* announcers are in the ring for two bouts each. This means that "advertising time" is longer when the TV viewership is highest. If the TV cameras come in for a closeup of the announcer giving water to a *yokozuna* before the final bout of the day, the name on the announcer's back will be in full view. It has been said that if a company name is on the screen for five seconds during the climactic bout on the last day of a tournament, it is worth two million yen in advertising. The financial output is definitely worthwhile.

Photographs

Having gone to the trouble of visiting the Kokugikan Hall, you will probably want to take a few pictures. In selecting your camera be careful to choose it with your seating position in mind, as it is virtually impossible to get a sharp close-up of two *rikishi* in a clinch from the far seats. The advantage of the balcony seats is that you can take good overall pictures of the hall. Regular lenses and compact cameras will allow you to frame shots that will adequately capture the atmosphere of Kokugikan. ISO 400 film will give you pictures with an even better impact value.

If you want shots of the *rikishi* themselves, the only way to do it is to camp out near the *hanamichi* aisles that the wrestlers use to enter the ring. This, too, has its drawbacks. That area can be very crowded and one more camera will only make it worse. *Rikishi* are extremely tense over their upcoming bouts and the crowd only agitates them more.

Stay for the Bow-twiring Ceremony

As soon as the final bout is over, the hall bustles with the preparations of the departing spectators. The program, however, is not yet over as the bow-twirling ceremony is still to come. This ceremony is performed by a *makushita rikishi*. He acts on behalf of the winning wrestlers, receiving the bow from the *gyoji*.

Some say the ceremony originated from the time of the *samurai* where the winner would receive a bow as an award. As a sign of thanks, the wrestler would then twirl the bow over his head and do a dance. Other explanations date this ceremony back to the age of sumo *sechie*.

This elegant finale is another aspect that sets sumo apart, helping make sumo the national sport. I might add, as a word to Japanese fans who are too busy to watch this special ceremony, that nearly all foreign spectators stay glued to their seats until the entire program is over.

The finale bout. Fans have their hands on their belongings, one foot in the aisle and eyes glued to the ring. The instant the bout ends, the stampede for the exits begins. It is not a pretty sight.

EVERYTHING IN SUMO BEGINS ON THE ROAD

Exhibition Sumo

There are 90 days of official sumo tournaments a year, but don't think the *rikishi* are taking it easy between bouts. They may have less free time than most regularly-employed businessmen. Between the six tournaments, *rikishi* have a heavy schedule of travel to exhibition tournaments, charity tournaments, retirement ceremonies, and so on. Of these, exhibitions are as grueling as regular tournaments.

Exhibitions are held four times a year; in spring, summer, October and December. Events are held in the Kanto and Kansai areas during the milder seasons. The summer exhibitions are held in the cooler north, and in the winter, wrestlers go to Kyushu where it is warmer than in other parts of Japan.

Rikishi travel from town to town, stopping in a different place each day to perform in a hall, gym, or school ground. It is a demanding schedule. Exhibitions, however, allow them to get closer to their fans and maintain the base of their popularity.

Rikishi would certainly rather take a rest after an official tournament, but they do their part to keep their sport in the public eye. As the exhibition bouts have no influence on their ranks, they are relaxed and the fans get a chance to see the warm human beings behind the stony faces usually seen on TV.

Yui Benefit Grand Sumo Exhibition Tournament

I had been planning to go to nearby Yokohama, but due to my lack of decisiveness I let the opportunity slip by, I didn't get another chance until the exhibition tournament at Yui took place, but by then I ended up taking a longer (and more expensive) trip than I had intended.

The last exhibition tournament in Yui had taken place thirty-six years before, and the excitement of the long-awaited event was palpable the instant I got off the train. The long line of people streaming out of the station were all families carrying packed lunches and thermoses, heading out to see sumo. The cars scouring the streets for parking spaces contained more of the same. Policemen, security officers, and even local fire fighters were busy conducting traffic. This was obviously a major event.

A Circus Tent?

The road leading to the junior high school where the day's sumo was to be held was lined with the banners bearing the *rikishi's* names. Looking closely, however, the sponsors printed on the banners were all local businesses. At exhibition matches these small-town big shots get their chances to be *tanimachi* sponsors.

I paid ¥5000 for my ticket, however exhibition ticket prices vary from place to place. As at the Kokugikan, I was able to get in without buying a ticket ahead of time. I was surprised to find that the exhibition tournament was to be held in what looked to be a circus tent. All it needed was a few big balloons flying overhead to complete the picture.

The grounds were full of people and it was only 8:30 a.m. The majority were junior high school students in their P.E. outfits, but there were also plenty of other people who had already staked out front row seats. The tent had been open since 7 a.m.! (Compared with 9 a.m. for official tournaments.)

The reason for the early start is that exhibition sumo starts out with the morning practice sessions. Fans get a chance to see a little bit of all aspects of sumo.

The *rikishi* had their usual training sessions: *Makushita*

on down started at 5 a.m., and by 7 or 8, the top wrestlers put in their appearances. This was a chance for fans to see sumo up close. For them, the training sessions of lower-ranked wrestlers were just as exciting as a bout between *yokozuna*. The thick columns usually used for pushing practice were missing, however the wrestlers went through other aspects of their training. Firstly, pairs of *rikishi* went through several bouts together. Then they lined up, with the first two *rikishi* facing off. The winner stayed on to fight the next *rikishi* and the loser returned to the line. They also demonstrated one form of training in which the top wrestlers lent their chests to the younger men for them to hit against. Some wrestlers even drew a circle in the sand on the playground to use as a practice ring. Everything at these events is a special treat.

Local Souvenir Stalls

While some people enjoyed the training sessions, others shopped at the souvenir stalls. Men tanned dark brown from outdoor work (fishermen?) were lined up to see the goods, their eyes aglow just like children at a festival, the only difference being their purchasing power. Some were buying ¥2500 telephone cards commemorating the retirement of Chiyonofuji, others were grabbing handfuls of ¥100 commemorative stamps at a booth set up outside the post office. (Japanese are slaves to their curiosity for anything new and unusual.)

Getting back to the stamps, they were unmistakably the bargain of the day at ¥100. The special-issue stamp was attached to a piece of paper listing the names of *yokozuna* through history. On this was the impression of a seal designed for the Yui event. The ¥100 price covered the stamp, but the post office must have lost money with the paper, printing, impression, and all the labor involved.

Other local specialties for sale included *sake*, fresh shrimp, and so on. It was a miniature industrial/agricultural fair. Exhibition sumo runs on a system that clearly benefits local enterprises.

Exhibitions are the Safari Parks of Sumo

I looked down to check the number of the seat stamped on my ticket, and when I looked back up, all I could see was skin. Mitoizumi, "The Salt Shaker," was standing right in front of me, and my range of vision was totally consumed by his bare back. You never know how big these guys are until you see them up close. You will also never know how intimidating they look until you find yourself gazing straight up into their faces. *Rikishi* are actually bigger and more muscular than they seem on TV.

Only at exhibitions will you get a chance to get a good view of the *makuuchi* wrestlers that you can only gaze at from afar at an official tournament. In fact, you will find them mingling with the crowd throughout the day. (If it is possible for such large creatures to "mingle.") This is part of the allure of local exhibitions.

Avid fans who never miss a day of sumo on TV are like city kids who drink milk at every meal but have no idea of what a cow really looks like.

It may be rude to create such a metaphor, but if official tournaments could be compared to a zoo, exhibitions are safari parks. This is literally live sumo. Before and after their bouts, wrestlers are relaxed. I saw Terao laughing and fooling around, and Akebono sweating profusely as he practiced his stamping over by the outdoor toilets. Some wrestlers were lighting up cigarettes. There is no better chance to find out what your favorite wrestler is really like.

Photo-op Heaven

The photographs I worked so hard to get at the Kokugikan were a breeze to obtain at the exhibition match. The abundancy of *rikishi* and the natural light created ideal conditions. There were a few *rikishi* who never came out of the dressing room for fear of being mobbed by ecstatic fans, but most readily agreed to having their pictures taken.

I saw one lady elbow into a shot only to turn to the people around her and ask, "Who was that sumo-*san*? Is he a champ?"

I saw one wrestler who was downright adorable in his embarrassment when a class of preschoolers asked him to pose with them.

Close-ups are no problem

Exhibition Sumo Fans are Serious

Most of the "seats" in the tent were *masu-seki*-style. A plastic sheet laid out on the floor had places marked out with masking tape. 1.5 square meters for four people. They were not as good as those at Kokugikan because the floor was harder and there were no hand rails. There were "guides" to show *masu-seki* holders their seats, but they were not employees of the Sumo Service Agency. The non-reserved chairs where I was sitting were as close to the ring as the Kokugikan "A" seats. This made the price of the seats more reasonable than I had first thought. My only complaint was with the lighting on the

Scenes like this are what make exhibitions fun

ring. As long as the sun was shining it was fine, but when clouds passed by, it was difficult to see the faces of the *rikishi*.

The fans were all very serious. The tent was 80% full when the low-ranking bouts began, and everyone paid strict attention. An entrance by any homegrown talent was greeted by cheers fit for a *yokozuna*. Every once in a while a cry would go up; it was usually a famous *rikishi* coming into the tent. When this happened, all the spectators would turn their attention from the ring to the direction where the ruckus had been raised. This sort of honest enthusiasm was also a pleasure to observe.

Announcers circled the hall selling original sumo souvenirs—towels for ¥200, gunbai for ¥500—and sales were brisk. Every fan wanted a souvenir of the day. Another big difference from official tournaments was that most of the fans packed their own lunches. I saw snacks, desserts, and picnic coolers full of drinks. It was almost like a school field day. There was no need for anyone to be on their best behavior lest they appear foolish in front of more knowledgable, seasoned spectators. All of the fans were sumo amateurs, happily relaxed and entertained. I saw one spectator toss an orange to a friend a few rows down; the atmosphere was definitely low-key.

Learning About Life from Sumo

There were schoolchildren in the seats behind me. The junior high school students all had a pamphlet prepared by their teachers entitled "Guide to Watching Grand Sumo." I asked the boy behind me to lend me his, and found it good reading. It included short descriptions of sumo history, rules, moves, spectator manners, information about the tea houses, and so on.

It was so interesting that I have included a selection here:

"Objective of Observation"

"Fierce ranking system and competition. Use this opportunity to find out firsthand the severe lifestyle and training of sumo wrestlers, and apply it to your own life. Today's event is a special observation activity. Do not just gape at the unusual aspects. Make serious observations of sumo and learn from it."

Sumo observation will serve to cultivate aesthetic sensitivity, this is obvious. I'm all in favor of using sumo bouts as lessons on life. But I finally decided that curios-

Teachers also want students to watch Sumo

ity at the unusual aspects would necessarily have to come before any great lesson filtered through. On the other hand I also realized that schools have to raise some sort of academic facade if they want to cut out classes for the day. Teachers never have it easy.

"Prohibited Activities During Observation Activities"

- •Shopping
- •Asking *rikishi* for autographs
- •Entering the dressing room

So this was the only way to keep the peace at exhibition tournaments. One had to conclude that shopping and autograph-hunting would make students too light-headed to learn anything. During the course of the day, however, I saw numerous teachers aiming their cameras at *rikishi* and many more students making a "peace" sign and worming themselves into shutter range. Surely nothing is better for learning, aesthetic or otherwise, than for teachers and students to enjoy themselves together.

I also learned that nobody can resist the allure of sumo.

Special Services

Exhibitions are a chance to see many things never shown at official tournaments: *jinku* (sumo folk songs), *shokkiri* (a comical sumo demonstration), drums, hairdressers, the tying of the ceremonial rope on the *yokozuna*, and so on. All of these special demonstrations have local sponsors.

All in all, fans have a chance to see the entire range of grand sumo in a single day. It seemed almost a better deal than going to the Kokugikan Hall.

The ring-entering ceremony was relaxed. Konishiki suddenly took the hand of a little girl in the crowd and circled the ring once with her. The crowd roared with delight. *Rikishi* seem to have a clear idea of their role in these special matches. I realized that the tent was full and some spectators were standing; fans had come from other cities in the area just to see sumo.

The exciting atmosphere made the time fly. Suddenly it was 3:30 and the day's program was over. Most of the equipment was already packed in the truck used for sumo tours. The match finished and the packing completed, the enormous entourage of 330 was back on the road.

The Sumo wrestler is also relaxed

179

The *rikishi* acted as goodwill ambassadors in London, but they were certainly doing no less during their domestic tours. The spectacle of the enthusiastic fans reacting open-heartedly to the *rikishi* visiting their hometown lent special meaning to the term "sumo—the national sport."

Other Sumo

Official tournaments and exhibition tours are not the only ways to see sumo; there are many others. If you cannot get tickets to see the official tournaments or travel to exhibitions, there are other events. Some are listed below, but you will need to consult sumo magazines for exact dates and times.

RETIREMENT SUMO

A wrestler who has managed to obtain elder stock will hold a haircutting ceremony which includes his installation as elder. To celebrate the event, bouts between wrestlers, *juryo* and above, are held. These occasions are like exhibition sumo in that you can see a *shokkiri* show, drum beating, sumo *jinku*, and so on. Retirement sumo is often held in the winter. It is easier than with a regular tournament to get *masu-seki* seats, except in the case of the retirement of a very popular *rikishi*.

TV-NETWORK SPONSORED TOURNAMENTS

Tournaments, held by brodcasting networks, are unique. NHK Sumo Benefit (end of January) includes a show of popular performers singing hit songs. The Fuji TV event (mid-February) gives away an enormous amount of prize money that is a powerful motivation for *rikishi*. TV Asahi has a benefit tournament at the end of September, and Nagoya TV sponsors the Sengoku Tomoesen after the Autumn Tournament. The Sumo Field Day is a humorous event that does not include bouts.

DEDICATION SUMO

Sumo is held at the Ise Shrine (in Mie Prefecture) in early April. It is also held at Yasukuni Shrine (Tokyo) at about the same time. These rituals highlight the religious aspects of the national sport. *Rikishi* aged 24 and 36 *(toshi-otoko)* throw beans for good luck at the Setsu-bun Ceremony on February 3 at Shinshoji Temple at Chiba's Naritasan.

STABLE SUPPORT GROUPS

SUMO WATCHING

If You Think You're in Love, Join a Stable Support Group

Most sumo stables have a support group system. In the deep, murky world of sumo you will not find any sales promotion, but there is a person in charge of such groups at each stable, and they will take requests any time.

The systems and fees are different for each stable. For example, there is one large stable that is home to several popular *makuuchi* wrestlers. They accept membership fees of ¥30,000 before each Tokyo tournament. Local support group branches collect fees for other tournaments.

Very few members join for only a single tournament. They are usually enthusiastic fans who stay on for the long term.

So what advantages are there in joining a support group? First of all, you can get seats for official tournaments. Supporters of the stable mentioned above receive two "A" seat tickets. For this alone the ¥30,000 fee is not unreasonable. Along with the tickets, members receive the ranking charts for each tournament, calendars, and so on. Some stables even put out a newsletter.

Another advantage is the chance to attend the party after the last day of a tournament. This is an opportunity open only to support group members.

A map showing the locations of stables and a list of addresses are included at the end of this section. Requests for support group information should be mailed in. Don't forget to include a stamped, self-addressed envelope for the reply.

You can also contact stables to find out about support groups for individual *rikishi*.

Going to See Training Sessions

As you find yourself getting in deeper, you will begin to wonder about the condition of your favorite *rikishi*. To find out, you'll have to visit morning training sessions *(keiko)*.

As a rule, training sessions are open to the public, but popular wrestlers tend to draw a crowd and the stable may turn people away. The rule for watching is silence. Training is different from tournament bouts. Always bear in mind that you have been given the privilege of observing.

GLOSSARY OF JAPANESE TERMS THAT APPEAR IN THIS BOOK

(All terms related to sumo ranks are
included in a chart on pages 43, 46, 189)

anko :   Angler fish. A component of the *chanko nabe* stew that wrestlers are raised on. Also used to describe wrestlers with a large, chunky physique.

banzuke :   The sumo ranking chart.

chanko nabe :   The one-pot meal wrestlers usually eat to gain weight.

chirichozu :   The motions a wrestler goes through when entering the ring for a bout. It has religious connotations and also shows opponents that he is unarmed.

chonmage :   A simple topknot hairstyle worn by all wrestlers *makushita* rank and below.

geta :   Japanese sandal-type footwear made of wood; worn by all new wrestlers of *jonokuchi* and *jonidan* ranks.

gunbai :   The gourd-shaped instrument held by sumo referees during bouts.

gyoji :   Sumo referee.

hakama :   Loose trousers worn over *kimono* worn by wrestlers *juryo*-rank and above.

hakata obi :   A type of sash worn with a semi-formal, cotton *kimono* by wrestlers *sandanme*-rank and above.

haori :   A loose-fitting jacket worn over their *kimono* by wrestlers *sandanme*-rank and above.

jinku :   Sumo folk songs.

joran sumo :   Command sumo performance before the Shogun.

kanjin sumo :   Sumo performed to raise money to re-build Buddhist temples; the purpose behind bouts held by the first professional wrestlers in the Edo era.

kensho :   Incentive prizes placed on individual tourna-ment bouts.

keiko :   Sumo training session.

kesho mawashi: Decorative aprons worn by *juryo*-rank wrestlers and above during ring-entering ceremony.

kinagashi :   Semi-formal, cotton *kimono* worn by wres-tlers *sandanme*-rank and above.

koenkai :   Sumo support/patron group.

kokugi :   "National Sport."

mage :   General term for all topknot hairstyles.

masu-seki: Box seats at the Kokugikan Hall.

mawashi :   Loincloth.

nakairi :   The portion of a day's tournament program

that includes the bouts of *maegashira* rank wrestlers and above.

obi : Sash worn with *kimono.*

oitcho : The "Big Gingko Leaf" hairstyle worn by wrestlers of *juryo*-rank and above.

oyakata : An honorific title for stablemasters, other retired wrestlers, and the top two referees.

rikishi : A sumo wrestler. The literal translation is "strong man."

sagari : The strands that hang from the tournament loincloths of wrestlers.

setta : Woven bamboo footwear worn by *sandanme* wrestlers and above.

shijuhatte : "48 hands." Refers to the original forty-eight winning sumo moves. Now is an adjective that roughly translates as "every trick in the book."

shikona : Wrestling name.

shokkiri : A comic sumo performance which demonstrates moves prohibited in regular bouts.

soppu : "Soup." Refers to the soup (more particularly the chicken carcass used to make the soup) for *chanko nabe* stew; also a term used to describe a wrestler with a lean, muscular physique.

sumobeya : Sumo stable.

sumo sechie : Sumo of the Nara and Heian eras, the outcome of which supposedly indicated the will of the gods concerning decisions national rulers had to make.

tabi :　Split-toed socks worn by high-ranking referees and wrestlers.

tamari-seki :　Seats immediately surrounding the sumo ring.

tanimachi :　A patron, supporter of a sumo stable or individual wrestler.

tate-gyoji :　Top two referees.

tenran sumo :　(See *joran sumo*.)

tsuji sumo :　Street sumo popular during the Kamakura era.

tsukibito :　A personal valet; a junior wrestler assigned to be at the beck and call of a wrestler of higher rank.

yobidashi :　An announcer.

yukata :　A simple cotton *kimono* worn by *jonokuchi* and *jonidan* wrestlers.

zori :　Bamboo sandles worn by high-ranking referees.

TABLE OF SUMO RANKS AND OTHER RELATED TERMS

yokozuna	Grand Champion. Wears the *yokozuna* rope to enter the ring. The only position from which a wrestler is never demoted.		These ranks are known collectively as *makuuchi*, or "Behind the Curtain." Bouts of *makuuchi* wrestlers are referred to as *nakairi*, or "entering the center."
ozeki *sekiwake* *komusubi*	"The Great Barrier" "Attendant to the Barrier" "Small Knot"	These three positions are collectively known as *sanyaku*, or "Three Officials."	
maegashira	"Front of the Head" Includes levels 1-16. Also known as *hiramaku*.		

juryo "Ten Ryo." The first salaried rank. Wrestlers from *juryo* on up are called by the honorific *sekitori*, or "Taker of the Barrier." *Juryo* is also the first rank where wrestlers are allowed to style their hair into the "Big Gingko Leaf" and wear *kesho mawashi* for the ring-entering ceremony.

makushita *sandanme* *jonidan* *jonokuchi*	"In Front of the Curtain" "The Third Step" "The Second Step of the Initial Stage" "The Initial Stage"	These are the unsalaried ranks, and there are no honorifics for referring to wrestlers therein. Bouts for these ranks are referred to collectively as *makushita* bouts.

MAP OF SUMO STABLES

1. Hanaregoma-beya
2. Futagoyama-beya
3. Minezaki-beya
4. Kise-beya
5. Kabutoyama-beya
6. Tatsutagawa-beya
7. Takasago-beya
8. Taiho-beya
9. Kitanoumi-beya
10. Oshiogawa-beya
11. Ajigawa-beya
12. Tomozuna-beya
13. Kasugano-beya
14. Izutsu-beya
15. Dewanoumi-beya
16. Oshima-beya
17. Tokitsukaze-beya
18. Tatsunami-beya
19. Nishonoseki-beya
20. Sadogatake-beya
21. Kataonami-beya
22. Wakamatsu-beya
23. Kokonoe-beya
24. Magaki-beya

25. Miyagino-beya
26. Azumazeki-beya
27. Mihogaseki-beya
28. Hakkaku-beya
29. Takadagawa-beya
30. Nakamura-beya
31. Kumagatani-beya
32. Asahiyama-beya
33. Kagamiyama-beya
34. Isenoumi-beya
35. Takashima-beya
36. Tamanoi-beya
37. Musashigawa-beya
38. Onaruto-beya
39. Naruto-beya
40. Matsugane-beya
41. Michinoku-beya
42. Isegahama-beya
43. Oguruma-beya
44. Minato-beya
45. Irumagawa-beya
46. Shikihide-beya
47. Hanakago-beya

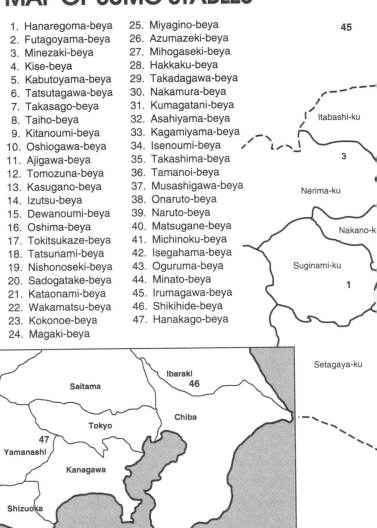

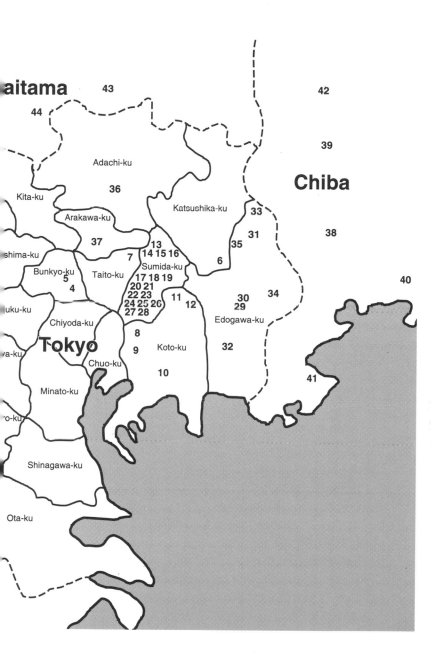

aitama

43

44

Adachi-ku

36

Kita-ku

Arakawa-ku

shima-ku

37

Bunkyo-ku

5

4

Taito-ku

13

14 15 16

7

Sumida-ku

17 18 19

20 21

22 23

24 25 26

27 28

11

12

Chiyoda-ku

8

Tokyo

9

Koto-ku

Chuo-ku

10

Minato-ku

Shinagawa-ku

Ota-ku

Katsushika-ku

33

31

35

6

30

29

34

Edogawa-ku

32

Chiba

42

39

38

40

41

LIST OF SUMO STABLES (1993)

Name of the stable master and his former name
and rank appear in parentheses.

Suginami-ku

1. Hanaregoma-beya 放駒部屋
     (Hanaregoma Teruyuki / *Ozeki* Kaiketsu)
     3-12-7 Asagaya-minami Suginami-ku Tokyo 166

Nakano-ku

2. Futagoyama-beya 二子山部屋
     (Futagoyama Toshiaki / *Ozeki* Takanohana)
     3-10-6 Hon-cho Nakano-ku Tokyo 164

Nerima-ku

3. Minezaki-beya 峰崎部屋
     (Minezaki Nobutake / *Maegashira* Misugiiso)
     2-20-3 Tagara Nerima-ku Tokyo 176

Bunkyo-ku

4. Kise-beya 木瀬部屋
     (Kimura Sehei / *Maegashira* Kiyonomori)
     2-35-21 Hongo Bunkyo-ku Tokyo 113

5. Kabutoyama-beya 甲山部屋
     (Kabutoyama Masaharu / *Maegashira* Daiyu)
     5-19-7 Hongo Bunkyo-ku Tokyo 113

Katsushika-ku

6. Tatsutagawa-beya 立田川部屋
     (Tatsutagawa Sakari / *Sekiwake* Aonosato)
     3-28-21 Shinkoiwa Katsushika-ku Tokyo 124

Taito-ku

7. Takasago-beya 高砂部屋
   (Takasago Uragoro / *Komusubi* Fujinishiki)
   1-16-5 Hashiba Taito-ku Tokyo 111

Koto-ku

8. Taiho-beya 大鵬部屋
   (Taiho Koki / *Yokozuna* Taiho)
   2-8-3 Kiyosumi Koto-ku Tokyo 135

9. Kitanoumi-beya 北の湖部屋
   (Kitanoumi Toshimitsu / *Yokozuna* Kitanoumi)
   2-10-11 Kiyosumi Koto-ku Tokyo 135

10. Oshiogawa-beya 押尾川部屋
    (Oshiogawa Takayoshi / *Ozeki* Daikirin)
    2-17-7 Kiba Koto-ku Tokyo 135

11. Ajigawa-beya 安治川部屋
    (Ajigawa Hiroaki / *Sekiwake* Mutsuarashi)
    1-7-4 Mouri Koto-ku Tokyo 135

12. Tomozuna-beya 友綱部屋
    (Tomozuna Takanori / *Sekiwake* Kaiki)
    1-20-7 Mouri Koto-ku Tokyo 135

Sumida-ku

13. Kasugano-beya 春日野部屋
    (Kasugano Terumasa / *Yokozuna* Tochinoumi)
    1-7-11 Ryogoku Sumida-ku Tokyo 130

14. Izutsu-beya 井筒部屋
    (Izutsu Akio / *Sekiwake* Tsurugamine)

2-2-7 Ryogoku Sumida-ku Tokyo 130

15. Dewanoumi-beya 出羽海部屋
(Dewanoumi Tomotaka / *Yokozuna* Sadanoyama)
2-3-15 Ryogoku Sumida-ku Tokyo 130

16. Oshima-beya 大島部屋
(Oshima Takeo / *Ozeki* Asahikuni)
3-5-3 Ryogoku Sumida-ku Tokyo 130

17. Tokitsukaze-beya 時津風部屋
(Tokitsukaze Katsuo / *Ozeki* Yutakayama)
3-15-3 Ryogoku Sumida-ku Tokyo 130

18. Tatsunami-beya 立浪部屋
(Tatsunami Osamu / *Sekiwake* Haguroyama)
3-26-2 Ryogoku Sumida-ku Tokyo 130

19. Nishonoseki-beya 二所ノ関部屋
(Nishonoseki Masahiro / *Sekiwake* Kongo)
4-17-1 Ryogoku Sumida-ku Tokyo 130

20. Sadogatake-beya 佐渡ケ嶽部屋
(Sadogatake Yoshikane / *Yokozuna* Kotozakura)
4-18-13 Taihei Sumida-ku Tokyo 130

21. Kataonami-beya 片男波部屋
(Kataonami Daizo / *Sekiwake* Tamanofuji)
1-33-9 Ishiwara Sumida-ku Tokyo 130

22. Wakamatsu-beya 若松部屋
(Wakamatsu Suehiro / *Ozeki* Asashio)
3-5-4 Honjo Sumida-ku Tokyo 130

23. Kokonoe-beya 九重部屋
(Kokonoe Mitsugu / *Yokozuna* Chiyonofuji)
4-22-4 Ishiwara Sumida-ku Tokyo 130

24. Magaki-beya 間垣部屋
(Magaki Katsuharu / *Yokozuna* Wakanohana)
3-8-1 Kamezawa Sumida-ku Tokyo 130

25. Miyagino-beya 宮城野部屋
(Miyagino Yasutaka / *Maegashira* Chikubayama)
4-16-3 Midori Sumida-ku Tokyo 130

26. Azumazeki-beya 東関部屋
(Azumazeki Daigoro / *Sekiwake* Takamiyama)
4-6-4 Higashi-komagata Sumida-ku Tokyo 130

27. Mihogaseki-beya 三保ケ関部屋
(Mihogaseki Noriaki / *Ozeki* Masuiyama)
3-2-12 Chitose Sumida-ku Tokyo 130

28. Hakkaku-beya 八角部屋
(Hakkaku Nobuyoshi / *Yokozuna* Hokutoumi)
1-16-1 Kamezawa Sumida-ku Tokyo 130

Edogawa-ku

29. Takadagawa-beya 高田川部屋
(Takadagawa Kazuichi / *Ozeki* Maenoyama)
2-1-15 Ichinoe Edogawa-ku Tokyo 132

30. Nakamura-beya 中村部屋
(Nakamura Yoshio / *Sekiwake* Fujizakura)
4-1-10 Chuo Edogawa-ku Tokyo 132

31. Kumagatani-beya 熊ケ谷部屋
(Kumagatani Taisuke / *Maegashira* Yoshinomine)
1-6-28 Minami-koiwa Edogawa-ku Tokyo 133

32. Asahiyama-beya 朝日山部屋
(Asahiyama Tadayuki / *Komusubi* Wakafutase)
4-14-21 Kita-kasai Edogawa-ku Tokyo 132

33. Kagamiyama-beya 鏡山部屋
(Kagamiyama Tsuyoshi / *Yokozuna* Kashiwado)
8-16-1 Kita-koiwa Edogawa-ku Tokyo 133

34. Isenoumi-beya 伊勢ノ海部屋
(Isenoumi Yukishige / *Sekiwake* Fujinokawa)
3-17-6 Harue-cho Edogawa-ku Tokyo 132

35. Takashima-beya 高島部屋
(Takashima Daizo / *Sekiwake* Koboyama)
3-21-2 Kami-ishiki Edogawa-ku Tokyo 133

Adachi-ku
36. Tamanoi-beya 玉ノ井部屋
(Tamanoi Tomoyori / *Sekiwake* Tochiazuma)
4-12-14 Umeda Adachi-ku Tokyo 123

Arakawa-ku
37. Musashigawa-beya 武蔵川部屋
(Musashigawa Akihide / *Yokozuna* Mienoumi)
4-27-1 Higashi-nippori Arakawa-ku 116

Chiba

38. Onaruto-beya 大鳴門部屋
    (Onaruto Hideyasu / *Sekiwake* Kotetsuyama)
    2-22-14 Kitakata Ichikawa-shi Chiba-ken 272

39. Naruto-beya 鳴門部屋
    (Naruto Toshihide / *Yokozuna* Takanosato)
    183 Hachigasaki Matsudo-shi Chiba-ken 270

40. Matsugane-beya 松ケ根部屋
    (Matsugane Mutsuo /*Ozeki* Wakashimazu)
    4-13-1 Kosaku-cho Funabashi-shi Chiba-ken 273

41. Michinoku-beya 陸奥部屋
    (Michinoku Yuji / *Maegashira* Hoshiiwato)
    4-23-18 Horie Urayasu-shi Chiba-ken 270-01

42. Isegahama-beya 伊勢ケ濱部屋
    (Isegahama Seinosuke / *Ozeki* Kiyokuni)
    225-9 Matsugasaki Kashiwa-shi Chiba-ken 277

Saitama

43. Oguruma-beya 尾車部屋
    (Oguruma Koichi / *Ozeki* Kotokaze)
    4-27-30 Inari Soka-shi Saitama-ken 340

44. Minato-beya 湊部屋
    (Minato Hiromitsu / *Komusubi* Yutakayama)
    2-20-10 Shibanakata Kawaguchi-shi Saitama-ken 333

45. Irumagawa-beya 入間川部屋
    (Irumagawa Tetsuo / *Sekiwake* Tochitsukasa)
    3-32-15 Hachioji Yono-shi Saitama-ken 338

Ibaraki

46. Shikihide-beya 式秀部屋
    (Shikimori Hidegoro / *Komusubi* Oshio)
    168-1 Aza Mokuda Sanuki-machi Ryugasaki-shi
    Ibaraki-ken 301

Yamanashi

47. Hanakago-beya 花籠部屋
    (Hanakago Tadaaki / *Sekiwake* Daijuyama)
    3956 Uenohara Uenohara-cho Kita-tsuru-gun
    Yamanashi-ken 409-01